Small Catechism

by Lois T. Kadel
Thomas E. Kadel
Richard Rehfeldt
Mark D. Tranvik
Larry Wohlrabe

Augsburg Fortress, Minneapolis

Contents ◆
Small Catechism

activities key

remembering (R)

seeking (S)

wandering (W)

hoping (H)

Creative Confirmation Series
Small Catechism

Writers: Lois T. Kadel and Thomas E. Kadel (Ten Commandments); Richard Rehfeldt (Lord's Prayer; Office of the Keys); Mark D. Tranvik (Catechism Basics; Apostles' Creed); Larry Wohlrabe (Sacraments).
Editors: Mary Nasby Lohre and Carolyn F. Lystig
Designer: Connie Helgeson-Moen
Cover Photographer: Jeff Greenberg/ AAA Stock Photos (front); © 1994 Jack Hamilton (back)

Scripture quotations unless otherwise noted are from New Revised Standard Version Bible, copyright 1989 Division of Christian Education of the National Council of the Churches of Christ in the United States of America. Used by permission.

Catechism quotations unless otherwise noted are from *A Contemporary Translation of Luther's Small Catechism: Study Edition*, copyright © 1994 Augsburg Fortress.

Materials identified as *LBW* are from *Lutheran Book of Worship*, copyright © 1978.

Introduction

CREATIVE CONFIRMATION

Welcome to the Creative Confirmation Series. This series invites you to customize a confirmation program that meets the needs of your youth and your congregation. These flexible confirmation resources work together through active and experiential learning activities to emphasize basic Bible literacy, the Small Catechism, worship, and daily life in the Christian community.

LEADER RESOURCES

Nine resource books are provided for pastors and leaders. *Bible 1, Bible 2, Bible 3,* and *Small Catechism* serve as the core of the program. The other five leader resources—*Worship, Community-Building Activities and Games, Sharing the Language of Faith, Mission/Service Projects,* and *Parent Conversations*—help you build a comprehensive confirmation program by providing related activities that nurture faith development in a community setting. The sessions are designed for a group of up to 12 middle school students.

LEARNER RESOURCES

Study Bible: The New Student Bible NRSV (Augsburg Fortress code 30-10-999) and *A Contemporary Translation of Luther's Small Catechism: Study Edition* (Augsburg Fortress code 15-5305) are the primary student resources for Creative Confirmation sessions. In some sessions a reproducible page from the leader resource is used. The *Youth Journal* guides learner reflection on many of the sessions in *Bible 1, Bible 2, Bible 3, Small Catechism, Worship,* and *Sharing the Language of Faith.* In session plans, look for the ✎ symbol and page number that point to a *Youth Journal* activity.

SMALL CATECHISM

This leader resource book for Creative Confirmation provides engaging activities that challenge youth and their leaders to explore the traditional teachings of the faith community in light of their own life experiences. This resource will help youth and their leaders:
- gain a basic understanding of Luther's Small Catechism;
- relate the parts of the catechism with contemporary issues of faith and life;
- explore their role in shaping the future of the faith community through their interpretation of the traditional teachings.

USING THIS RESOURCE

Each of the 34 sessions in this book is designed to last about 20 minutes. Within a single learning period, churches can group more than one catechism session or combine a single catechism session with activities from the other resource books.

If you are responsible for the entire class time, matching the symbol included in each session will guide you in selecting activities from the other resource books. (See the key on the contents/credits page.) If an activity does not have a symbol, it can be used in any session.

> Engaging activities challenge youth and their leaders to explore traditional teachings of the faith community in light of their life experiences.

A Need for Reform

FOCUS Five hundred years ago the church needed to be reformed because it was teaching that people could earn God's love.

BACKGROUND In 1500, the continent of Europe was dramatically different from the one we know today. Frightful diseases were common; during the 14th century, the plague wiped out almost half of Europe's population. If a person was fortunate enough to survive childbirth, he or she could expect to live only to the age of 40. Only a small percentage of people could read.

The Roman Catholic Church was the only church of significance. This powerful church was headed by the pope; yet, many cracks and strains were beginning to exist beneath its polished surface.

Late medieval theology taught that it was up to the individual to initiate a saving relationship with God, a relationship that would put worries about the after-life to rest. As a result, men and women were left wondering whether they had "done enough" to satisfy God. This led people to try to do something like fasting or taking a pilgrimage to earn God's love and a place in heaven.

◆ More information is available in the introductory pages of *A Contemporary Translation of Luther's Small Catechism: Study Edition.*
◆ Reproducible Page 1 may be used with "A Need for Reform."
◆ Reproducible Page 2 may be used with each of the sessions in "Catechism Basics."

WARM-UP Distribute markers and paper. Have each person draw a picture of the vehicle used most often by his or her family. Then each person should ask, "How is this vehicle like my family?" Encourage everyone to think of as many similarities as possible, such as:
◆ Some cars have four wheels. How many family members are in your family?

◆ Are there rusty spots or squeaky parts in your family?
◆ What radio stations are tuned in and how do they represent your family's voice/voices?

Then have them ask themselves, "If my family were to receive a tune up, what things do I think could use a little extra attention or work?"

ACTIVITY The Bible speaks of Christians as being part of the same family, the church. Martin Luther thought highly of this church family and valued being a part of it. However, Luther recognized at the time of the Reformation that the church family was in desperate need of help. Divide the class into smaller groups and study these questions.

1. What needed repair in the church family? *(The teaching that we must do something to earn God's love.)*

2. What was wrong about this teaching? *(See Ephesians 2:8. God's love in Christ comes to us first.)*

3. What can happen when we try to earn God's love? *(See Romans 7:23-24. We end up at war with ourselves because we want to do what is right because we love God, not because we are trying to earn God's love. We know God loves us, regardless of what we do.)*

4 Can you point to some times when you tried to earn God's love or get God on your side? *(Note ways we bargain with God—for good grades, for recovery from illness, and so forth.)*

RESPONSE Pray together the prayer for "The Church" as found on page 45 of *Lutheran Book of Worship.*

Catechism Basics
God's Forgiveness

FOCUS   Martin Luther discovers God's forgiveness.

BACKGROUND   Martin Luther was born in Germany in 1483. He began preparing to be a lawyer, largely at the urging of his father. A near-death experience in a thunderstorm in 1505 led Luther to enter a monastery. While there, Luther earned his doctor's degree in theology in 1512. As a monk, Luther's chief concern was to save himself.

The church of the day taught that a person must initiate a relationship with God before God would bestow the grace necessary to save. Luther felt he had never done enough to merit God's love and favor, no matter how much he fasted, read the Bible, or confessed his sins. Luther discovered in the Bible that God's love exists prior to any of our good works. Jesus Christ died to forgive our sins, and that act alone is sufficient to warrant our inclusion in God's kingdom. He found Paul's teaching that we are justified by faith and not by works of the law to be tremendously freeing.

Armed with this new understanding of Christ and God's Word, Luther challenged the view of the established church in Rome. In 1517, he nailed his 95 Theses to the church door in Wittenberg. He declared that the Roman church's selling of indulgences (slips of paper that forgave sins) was contrary to Scripture. Many people agreed with Luther, and a significant movement to renew the church was born. We know that movement as the Reformation.
- More information is available in the introductory pages of *A Contemporary Translation of Luther's Small Catechism: Study Edition.*
- Reproducible Page 2 may be used with each of the sessions in "Catechism Basics."

WARM-UP   Before the day of class, ask everyone to assemble personal time capsules. These should include items that represent significant moments in their lives, items like: a baptismal certificate, a baseball from a big league game they attended, sheet music from a recital, or a souvenir from a vacation. (People may draw the items on 3" x 5" cards if they were unable to bring them to class.) As they arrive, ask them to identify the items in their time capsules and explain each item's significance.

ACTIVITY   Tell them to listen carefully as you tell a story so they will be able to retell it afterwards. After you have shared the information in the "Background" with them, place the following items in the middle of the room. Provide an umbrella, bread and water, hammer and nail, and a sign that says: "FOR SALE: FORGIVENESS OF SINS." Invite volunteers to explain how each item fits into the story. (*Answers: The umbrella stands for the thunderstorm, the bread and water for the fasting, the hammer and nail for the nailing of the 95 Theses, and the sign for the selling of indulgences.*)

Use these questions to check their understanding of the story.

1. What made Luther enter the monastery? (*A near-death experience in a thunderstorm.*) What happened to him there? (*He discovered God's forgiveness.*)

2. How did he protest the sale of indulgences? (*He nailed the 95 Theses to the church door.*)

3. How is the love of a parent for a child like God's love for us? (*See Luke 15:11-24; it is a love that disciplines but does not reject or shame.*)

RESPONSE   Pray together the prayer for "Renewal" as found on page 47 of *Lutheran Book of Worship.*

Catechism Basics

Teaching the Truth

FOCUS Luther was able to reform the church because a large number of people believed he was teaching the truth about the Bible.

BACKGROUND Martin Luther's spark of protest soon grew into a roaring inferno. In 1521 Luther was called to the German city of Worms and asked to denounce his teaching. Luther refused and narrowly escaped with his life. He was declared an enemy of the Roman Catholic Church and a price was put on his head. However, Luther's arguments about Christ's all-sufficient victory on the cross and the inability of men and women to save themselves made sense to many people. Furthermore, the people were tired of the way bishops and other clergy seemed to be enriching themselves while their poor parishioners remained uncertain about their final destiny. Consequently, Luther was protected and the movement gained steam. Centered in Wittenberg, Luther and his followers preached, wrote, and taught about Christ's love for the ungodly. By the 1530s, wide areas of northern Europe were won over to the Lutheran faith.

A final attempt to heal the breach between Luther's followers and Rome occurred at the German city of Augsburg in 1530. However, by this time the two sides were too far apart. One result of this meeting was the Augsburg Confession, a summary of the Lutheran understanding of the Bible that remains authoritative for Lutherans today. Luther lived out his later years preaching and teaching the gospel and urging the reform of the church in accordance with God's Word. He was married in 1525 to Katherine von Bora, a former nun. They had six children together. He died in 1546 and is generally recognized to be one of the most influential people in history.

◆ More information is available in the introductory pages of *A Contemporary Translation of Luther's Small Catechism: Study Edition.*

◆ Reproducible Page 2 may be used with each of the sessions in "Catechism Basics."

WARM-UP Distribute markers and paper and whatever art supplies you have available. Make greeting cards to celebrate the Reformation. Use poetry and designs to communicate what the Reformation was about and why we should observe it. If this activity is done close to Reformation Sunday (the last Sunday in October), post the cards in a public place or mail them to family or friends.

ACTIVITY Divide the class into two groups. Invite two good readers to come and read silently the "Background" information for this session. Then have them go back and tell their groups as much as they can remember about what they have read. When they are done, have the two volunteers remain silent while you pose the following questions to the rest of the class to see how much of the story they learned.

1. What happened at the city of Worms? *(Luther was asked to take back his teachings.)*

2. Why wasn't Luther executed as a criminal? *(His teaching was popular, so he was protected.)*

3. Why did Luther refuse to be silent and obey his church? *(Luther believed that the teachings of the Bible and Christ were above all human authority.)*

4. Why do you think Romans 3:28 was one of Luther's favorite verses? *(This verse says good works do not put us right with God.)*

5. Why are Luther's teachings still needed in the church today? *(People still think they need to do something to earn God's love—be popular, have a lot of money, pray in the "right" way, and so forth.)*

RESPONSE Pray together the prayer for "Teachers" as found on page 46 of *Lutheran Book of Worship.*

Catechism Basics

The Basics of Faith

FOCUS   Martin Luther wrote the Small Catechism in order to teach Christians the basics of the faith.

BACKGROUND   Martin Luther wrote many books, but the Small Catechism was one of his favorites. The church bearing his name has echoed this sentiment and made the Small Catechism a staple of confirmation instruction for more than 400 years. Luther wrote this teaching tool in the late 1520s, after he visited some churches in the area of Wittenberg with other leaders of the Reformation and saw that the common people were in desperate need of a basic guide to the Christian faith.

Luther put the Ten Commandments first, followed by the Apostles' Creed, the Lord's Prayer, and the Sacraments of Baptism and Holy Communion. This order reflected Luther's belief that through the Law, the Commandments, we learn to dismiss any possibility of saving ourselves. Then we are ready to receive the mercy of Christ as contained in the Creed and the Lord's Prayer. The sacraments reinforce this by talking about how Christ comes in the midst of our daily lives and nurtures our faith.

Down through the ages the gentle rhythms of the Small Catechism have nurtured countless Christians in the fundamentals of the faith. Those who make it their own have a companion to treasure until they are reunited with Christ.

♦ More information is available in the introductory pages of *A Contemporary Translation of Luther's Small Catechism: Study Edition.*

♦ Reproducible Page 2 can be used with each of the sessions in "Catechism Basics."

WARM-UP   Find one or two older members of your congregation for whom the catechism has been a vital part of their faith and life. Invite them to class so they can tell about how they learned the catechism and how it might have been used in their homes. Let them tell how parts of the catechism have spoken deeply

to them at various stages of their lives. Be sure to allow time for the group to ask them questions about the catechism. (This lesson is also a good opportunity to link young persons with older members who can serve as "catechists" for the confirmation program. This is also an excellent way to build relationships between the generations.)

ACTIVITY   Write the following questions on the chalkboard or chart paper as each person finds a partner. Distribute a pencil and a paper to each pair, and have them listen for the answers as you share the information in the "Background" with them. When you are done, have the pairs exchange papers and check answers as you review the following questions. Remind them to be "grace-ful" as they read each other's work.

1. Why did Luther write the Small Catechism? *(He saw that people did not know the basics of the Christian faith.)*

2. What basics of faith are covered in the catechism, and what order is followed? *(Commandments, Creed, Lord's Prayer, Baptism, and Holy Communion.)*

3. Why is the catechism ordered this way? *(The Commandments reveal our need of a Savior. The Creed and the Lord's Prayer present the Savior. The sacraments make Jesus present for us.)*

4. Why is it important to know something about God and Jesus? *(Then we know the depth of God's love for us and we can tell others about God and Christ.)*

5. When did you remember or think about God during this past week?

RESPONSE   Pray together the prayer for "Guidance" as found on page 49 of *Lutheran Book of Worship.*

Ten Commandments
First Commandment

FOCUS   The freedom to be human comes from acknowledging God as God. The key word is *freedom.*

BACKGROUND   God says in the First Commandment, "You shall have no other gods." While this may seem to restrict us, it actually gives us a great freedom. False gods derive their power from us. When we substitute other things or people as our gods, we must also assume the responsibility for keeping those gods in first place. However, when the living God is in first place, we don't have to be perfect. We have the freedom to be human—that is, we do not have to be anything we are not.

WARM-UP   Begin to read the following paragraph about the Ten Commandments as the students call out words they think fit in the blank spaces. Then read the paragraph with the students' chosen words in the blanks. The students will decide by vote whether the each sentence is true.

"Today we are beginning our study of the ___ _____. We will see how each of the Commandments is actually a gift of ___ to us. It is all too easy to let _____ gods rule our lives, but the _____ God knows that this takes away our freedom. ___ gives us the Commandments as a gift of love."

Then write the correct words on a chalkboard or chart paper. The words are listed consecutively as they appear in the above paragraph: *Ten; Commandments; God; pretender; living; God.* Now reread the paragraph and allow the group to fill in the blanks with the correct words.
- ◆ See Reproducible Page 3 for an alternate "Warm-up" activity.

ACTIVITY   Introduce the activity by noting:
- ◆ Not everything in a person's life has the same importance for that person. Most things fit into one of these categories: things that don't matter much; things that are important, but not essential; and things that are essential. Some things *seem* important, but they are not. In this activity, we will call them "pretender gods."
- ◆ A pretender god is anything that we believe can give us what we believe we need. Some pretender gods might be: money, cars, or even people.

Give the group three minutes to list as many pretender gods as they can on a piece of paper. Then ask them to read the lists to the group. As each pretender god is named, ask the group:

1. How does this pretender god seem to give people freedom?

2. How does this pretender god really take freedom away from people?"

RESPONSE   Read aloud the First Commandment and Luther's explanation of it on page 13 of *A Contemporary Translation of Luther's Small Catechism.* Encourage group discussion by having class members discuss the following questions. If the group is larger than four people, break the class into smaller groups.

1. Why is God so concerned that we have no other gods?

2. Is this a commandment that restricts our enjoyment of life or expands our enjoyment of life? Why?

3. Why do you think this commandment comes first?

Ten Commandments

Second Commandment

FOCUS When we keep God's name precious to us, we are not tempted to forget that God is precious to us and that God's power is given to us. The keyword is *power.*

BACKGROUND Whenever we treat something lightly, we devalue it and lose a sense of its uniqueness. Of all things, this applies most to God's name. We don't damage God when we misuse God's name; instead, we damage our awareness of what God has made available to us through Jesus Christ and the Holy Spirit. To treat God's name lightly or to misuse it, can easily dull us to the wonder, majesty, and power that stands behind that name.

WARM-UP When the students have gathered, ask them to name some things that we take for granted, but things that might be considered priceless by someone else. As items are named, list them on the chalkboard or chart paper.

Once a few things have been named, ask them to name some things that we might consider priceless, but that someone else in the world might take for granted. Point out how something may have one value in one circumstance and quite a different value in another circumstance.

ACTIVITY Begin by asking the group to list on the chalkboard or chart paper words that describe their concepts of what power is. Focus the request by asking how power is understood in the comics, on TV, in professional sports, and in their homes.

To help group members note common ways of making light of or sapping another's power, pose the following scenario. Read it sincerely the first time. Then, read it sarcastically.

The team is gathered just before the big game. The coach says to them, "Okay, team, listen up. This is the big game. You need to know that our opponents have lightening speed and stunning quickness. They've hammered everyone lately. Now we're going to go out there like the plodders they think we are. I'm sure they don't believe we can score against them. We probably can't, you know what I mean? Just try to finish the game before they hurt us, okay?"

Ask the group to comment on how the very same word can have two different meanings, depending on the way it is used. Note that our words can affect how we think about something or someone. Invite students to provide some examples from the scenario, and also from their experiences.

RESPONSE Read the Second Commandment and Luther's explanation of it to the group. Find it on page 14 of *A Contemporary Translation of Luther's Small Catechism.* Ask everyone to listen carefully. Then, use the following questions to encourage participants to explore their understanding of the commandment.

1. When was the last time you "made wrongful use" of something? What do those words mean in that context, and what do you think they mean in this commandment? Why do you think people use swear words? How do those words make people feel when they use them?

2. Why do you think God made this commandment? How are we supposed to handle things that are sacred? Does this commandment end up benefiting us in some way?

 See corresponding activity in the *Youth Journal,* page 40.

Ten Commandments
Third Commandment

FOCUS When we set aside certain times to relax, rest, and reflect on God's Word, we become aware of the special nature of all time as a gift from God. The keyword is *time*.

BACKGROUND From the beginning of God's special relationship with us, God has desired that we experience a special time as a regular part of our lives. We call this special time the Sabbath. Although in Luther's Small Catechism he limits his focus to the hearing of God's Word, he elsewhere notes that the Sabbath is not a particular day of the week or a particular way to spend the day. Rather, it is special time—a time to focus on our relationship with God and from that, our relationship with other people.

WARM-UP When all have arrived say without explanation, "Wait a minute." Indicate with a gesture that no one is to speak, and also remain silent for the next 60 seconds.

When the minute has ended, ask the participants how that minute made them feel. Then say, "Today we will think about time. Time is another gift from God. The Third Commandment is about time. It is about a special time that God calls the Sabbath."

ACTIVITY Ask each person to find a partner. Give each pair two copies of Reproducible Page 4 so they have 168 Time Bucks. (*The Time Bucks can be photocopied or they can be imaginary.*) Each pair is to be given 10 minutes to spend their Time Bucks in the way that they think is best. There are 168 hours in a week. The Time Bucks are for 5, 10, and 30 minutes; and for 1, 2, 3, and 4 hours. They should apportion their Time Bucks into the following categories:

Rest	School/Study	Friends
Eating	God	Chores
Grooming	TV/radio/music	Family
Other	Other	Other

When the allotted time has expired, ask the participants to comment on the way they spent their Time Bucks. Are they comfortable with the time they allotted to God?

RESPONSE Read aloud the Third Commandment and Luther's explanation of it on page 15 of *A Contemporary Translation of Luther's Small Catechism*. Then ask participants to share their thoughts on the following questions. If you have more than six participants, break the class into smaller groups for this discussion.

1. Have you and your parents ever had a conversation about the way you spend your time? Why do you think God made this commandment? What happens to people who work or play all the time?

2. If we were to rename the Sabbath "Special Time," what is it that would make it special for you, your friends and family, and for all people?

3. Does God want to structure whatever free time we presently have, or is there another reason that God commands that we observe sabbath time? What happens to the relationship between a person and God if they never spend any time together?

The Ten Commandments

Fourth Commandment

Honor, esteem, and respect are basic building blocks of all healthy relationships—especially our first relationships with our parents. The keyword is *honor.*

BACKGROUND The word *honor* means to hold in esteem, to value, or to show respect. Honor is a basic component of all healthy relationships. In the Fourth Commandment, God prepares us for all relationships by establishing that honor, esteem, and respect be the basis for one's primary relationship with his or her parents.

This brief experience with the Fourth Commandment does not permit a look into the abusive uses of authority and parenthood. The leader should be sensitive to the possibility that one or more students in the class may have been subjected to some form of abuse by parents or others in authority.

WARM-UP You will need one single-lettered file card for each participant. Depending upon the size of the class, you will need to select which word or words to use for this activity. The cards with single letters will spell out one or more of the following key words: HONOR, RESPECT, ESTEEM. (If you have a large group, use a different colored marker for each chosen word.) As the participants arrive, give each one a file card with a letter on it. Tell them to try to figure out what word or words the letters spell.

ACTIVITY Ask everyone to stand. Have each person, in turn, suggest one example of honor from their experiences or from something they have read or watched. As they do so, have them be seated.

Then, read aloud the Fourth Commandment and Luther's explanation of it on page 16 of *A Contemporary Translation of Luther's Small Catechism.* Have them replace the word *honor* with the word *respect* when they read the commandment. Issue the following invitation to the group: Let's see if we can begin to figure out why God would devote a whole commandment to honoring and respecting parents.

Tell the group that you are going to define the corners of the room, have them stand again, and read them some statements. One corner will be the I AGREE CORNER; another corner will be the I DISAGREE CORNER; the third corner will be the I DON'T KNOW CORNER; and the fourth corner will be the I WANT TO EXPRESS AN IDEA CORNER.

Invite the group to stand. Tell them that as you read the statements, each person is to go to the corner that best expresses his or her feelings about the statement. If one or more persons go to the I WANT TO EXPRESS AN IDEA CORNER, assure them they will be given time to say what they want to say.

Statements:

1. The first relationship most people experience is with parents or persons who do the child's parenting.

2. No parents are perfect parents.

3. Honor and respect are basic parts of all healthy relationships.

4. Parents should deserve honor and respect before their children need to show it.

5. If we can somehow have a healthy relationship with parents, we are far more likely to be able to have healthy relationships with others.

RESPONSE Divide everyone into three groups: the PARENTS' GROUP, the CHILDREN GROUP, and the GOD GROUP. Give each group time to discuss the question and prepare an answer that reflects the perspective named in the group. When everyone is ready, ask each group to share its response to the question. Allow time for discussion.

Discuss the following questions: Why do you think God put this commandment first in the group of the commandments that deal with how we are to treat other people? How are parents alike or different from God?

Ten Commandments
Fifth Commandment

FOCUS When we respect life, we prize it and cherish it. The keyword is *life.*

BACKGROUND Martin Luther's insight into this commandment is shown in his explanation, which goes well beyond a simple directive not to kill other people. Luther indicates that this commandment also provides us the command that we help others live.

This brief encounter with the Fifth Commandment will focus on respect for life and how God's commandment not to kill is actually the gift of freedom to prize and cherish all life.

WARM-UP As people arrive, ask them to figure out how many days they have been alive. Be ready to provide assistance to those who are less comfortable with the multiplication and addition that this activity requires. A calculator might be a handy tool to have. You might mention that if a person lives to be 70 years old, that person will have lived more than 25,550 days!

ACTIVITY Bring one or two recent newspapers to class. Have group members work in pairs. Give each pair a section of the newspaper and tell them to find examples of murdering. Remind them that murdering the physical body is only one way of killing a person. What other kinds of examples can they find?

Then reassemble the group and ask the pairs to report their findings. With each report ask,

"What is being murdered in that report?" (*In some cases, the report may be about murdering the body. Other kinds of murdering might include: murdering a person's ability to live in peace; murdering a person's hope; murdering a person's dream; or murdering a person's sense of security.*)

Read aloud the Fifth Commandment and Luther's explanation of it on page 17 in *A Contemporary Translation of Luther's Small Catechism.* Emphasize that this commandment means that we are not only to refrain from all these various ways of murdering, but also to respect and cherish life so much that we try to help others in meeting all their important needs. Referring to the examples found in the newspaper, ask them to think of ideas for helping some of these people live. Ask them to share what they think God's people might be able to do.

RESPONSE After people have had an opportunity to share thoughts and opinions about the examples they have found ask them, "Can we discover anything about God from the fact that this commandment is so important to God that it made the list of 10 that God has given us?"

 See corresponding activity in the *Youth Journal*, page 41.

Sixth Commandment

FOCUS When we are faithful to our partners, we contribute to their well-being and to the well-being of our family and our community. The keyword is *partnership*.

BACKGROUND Families are the foundation of community, and partnership is the foundation of the family. In families headed by partners who are committed and faithful to one another, there is a sense of well-being in which openness, trust, and confidence flourish. These families, in turn, are far more likely to contribute to the well-being of the larger community. In this session, we will look at the concept of partnership as a gift from God that, when honored, becomes a fundamental way that God blesses all people.

WARM-UP Do a trust walk. When all have arrived, ask each person to find a partner. In each partnership, one person will close his or her eyes and be guided around the room by the other. After three or four minutes, the partners switch roles and repeat the experience.

ACTIVITY Reflect on the trust walk. Ask class members to talk about their experience with it using the following discussion guide.
- Was it easy to entrust yourself to your partner?
- Were you able to keep your eyes closed the whole time that you were being guided around the room?
- Did you like this experience or did you find it uncomfortable?

Help the group take a look at partnership. Ask them what qualities a good partnership must have. Write the responses on the chalkboard or newsprint.

Read aloud the Sixth Commandment and Luther's explanation of it on page 18 of *A Contemporary Translation of Luther's Small Catechism*. Remind everyone that the Sixth Commandment begins with the words "You shall not." Have them restate the commandment by identifying desirable behavior. This time, begin it by saying, "You shall . . ."

RESPONSE Lead a discussion on the Sixth Commandment using some or all of the following discussion starters.

1. Why do you think that God gave this commandment to us? How does this commandment help us understand how we are to use God's gift to us of sexuality?

2. What does this commandment have to do with the word *partnership?* How does *faithfulness* fit into this idea? What happens when trust is broken?

3. Do you think that the benefits of this commandment reach beyond the partners themselves? What about their children? What about the larger community?

Ten Commandments

Seventh Commandment

When we treat others with fairness and justice, we enhance their opportunity to live lives that contribute to the general welfare. The keyword is *justice.*

BACKGROUND This commandment specifically mentions stealing, but in a broader sense seeks to protect a person's ability to live a secure and productive life. The Seventh Commandment introduces this concept and the Eighth through Tenth Commandments continue to sharpen its implications.

When a person is helped by neighbors and lives a productive life, that person contributes to the well-being of the community as well as his or her personal well-being. Like the other commandments, this one seeks to strengthen the whole community as well as protect one person from another.

WARM-UP As everyone arrives, ask group members to interview each other about any experiences they have had with robbery. The interviewers should find out what was stolen and how it felt to be robbed. Allow a few minutes for the brief interviews. Then ask each pair to report to the whole class about their interview.

ACTIVITY Duplicate Reproducible Page 5 for use in this activity. Divide everyone into two groups. Announce that the groups will compete against each other in a contest based upon the Bible passage. The first group to answer each question correctly will receive five points. Give Group A a copy of Ephesians 4:25—5:2; give Group B a copy of Ephesians 4:25—5:2 with many of the words missing. The questions follow:

1. From what book of the Bible does this passage come?

2. According to Ephesians 4:25, what are we to put away?

3. According to Ephesians 4:29, what should you not let come out of your mouth?

4. According to Ephesians 4:30, what should you avoid doing to the Holy Spirit?

5. According to Ephesians 5:1, what are we to be?

6. According to Ephesians 5:2, what kind of offering should we be?

When Group A wins (as it should), ask Group B why it did so poorly in the competition. *(Group members will probably say that the quiz wasn't fair, since they didn't have all the words.)* Agree with them and confess that many answers were "stolen" or taken away from Group B's copy of the Bible passage.

Read aloud the Seventh Commandment and Luther's explanation of it on page 19 in *A Contemporary Translation of Luther's Small Catechism.* Highlight the following words in it: . . . *but help them to improve and protect their property and income.* Note that when things are stolen from us, it means that those things are not available to help us.

Now ask the group why they think God included the Seventh Commandment in the list of Commandments.

RESPONSE Use these questions to guide a group discussion.

1. Have any of you ever had anything stolen from you? How did it make you feel?

2. Does one generation ever steal from another?

3. Can you think of any kinds of theft that don't affect someone in some fashion?

4. What should you do if you know that someone has stolen something?

 See corresponding activity in the *Youth Journal,* page 42.

Ten Commandments
Eighth Commandment

FOCUS   Our words have enormous power to build a person up or tear a person down. In this commandment, God expresses the importance of building up and strengthening others. The keyword is *relationship*.

BACKGROUND   Most young people (and adults, too, for that matter) have little appreciation for how much power their words have. Words have the power to hurt people or help them. In this commandment, God seeks to protect us from the destructive power of words. Even more than that, the Eighth Commandment leads us to acknowledge and make good use of the positive power of our words. When our words speak the truth, we contribute to the well-being and safety of others. Healthy relationships are based upon truth.

WARM-UP   As people arrive, ask them to see how many different words they can make out of the letters in the word *relationship*.

ACTIVITY   Announce to the group that you are going to describe someone. After the description, ask the group to figure out how this young man would be treated at their school.

Description 1: He is tall and gangly. He wears unusual clothes. No one thinks he is handsome. Some even say his appearance is grotesque. He was born far away, and his parents never finished elementary school. He has moved often, so he hasn't learned much in school. He's used to being called names because people seem to enjoy making fun of him. He seems depressed most of the time.

Following their remarks, tell the group to listen to another description and predict this person's treatment at their school.

Description 2: He is very, very strong. When he makes up his mind about what is right, he goes for it without worrying about the consequences of his actions. He is a very good public speaker. Some have described him as a calm person with high morals and a lot of smarts. Others have described him as a real winner.

Again, when all group members have had an opportunity to share their ideas, explain that both descriptions were of the same person and that the person was Abraham Lincoln.

Now ask the group to comment on how the words we use to describe a person can make the difference between that person's acceptance or rejection. This is the focus of the Eighth Commandment: *Words have the power to build up or to destroy a person.* Read to the class the Eighth Commandment and Luther's explanation of it on page 20 of *A Contemporary Translation of Luther's Small Catechism.*

RESPONSE   Ask group members to share their ideas about why God cares about what people say about each other. Find out: What opportunities do we have to speak well of others. When is advertising a false witness? What do your friends know about your relationship with God from the way you speak?

Encourage everyone to remember that God is a God of relationships. Speaking positively about a person is not only kind to that person, but it helps build and maintain good and strong relationships between people in a community.

Ten Commandments
Ninth Commandment

Respect for our neighbor's property protects that person's property and permits us to be joyful about what we have received from God. The keyword is *respect.*

 BACKGROUND The word *covet* literally means to desire earnestly. While the group may see little wrong with desiring something, this commandment speaks to the kind of desiring that imprisons a person.

The opposite of coveting could be thought of as respecting. To respect another's property is to honor the boundaries between what belongs to me and what belongs to the other. Only in this way can we truly recognize and be grateful for what God has given us.

WARM-UP Find the key word on Reproducible Page 6. Make and distribute copies of this page and instruct the students to work in pairs and use a Bible to answer the questions. Tell them that the number for each answer corresponds to a letter in the alphabet. For instance: 1 = A, 6 = F, and so forth. See who can find the key word first. (The key word is: *RESPECT.*)

ACTIVITY Make up a story together. Have members of the group arrange themselves in a circle. (If your group is larger than eight, form two or more groups.) Tell them that you want the group to make up a story after you supply the first line. Each person, in turn, will supply one new line to the story. The activity is concluded when the story telling has gone around the circle two times. The last person should contribute a story ending.

The first line of the story is: *Once upon a time, there was a couple who had a very nice house, but they thought their neighbor's house was bigger and better.*

Following the story making, ask group members to explain some key points of the story they created.

◆ What did the couple do? Did they try to get their neighbor's house? Did they succeed?
◆ What happened to their own house while they yearned for their neighbor's house?

Help the group relate the story to the Ninth Commandment. Read aloud the Ninth Commandment and Luther's explanation of it on page 21 of *A Contemporary Translation of Luther's Small Catechism.* Whether their story seems to follow or contradict the commandment, tease the commandment's implications out of the story the students constructed.

RESPONSE Ask the group how God helps our neighbor by making a commandment that tells us not to covet our neighbor's property. Find out: What possessions do participants envy most? Where does that envy come from? Does this mean we should support the unequal distribution of the world's resource?

After some ideas are shared, ask everyone to react to the following statement: *I am free to experience joy in God's gifts to me only after I have developed respect for what God has given to my neighbor.*

Ten Commandments
Tenth Commandment

FOCUS Our neighbor is strengthened by the loyalty of family, friends, and others. The keyword is *loyalty*.

 BACKGROUND The Tenth Commandment and the afterword to the Ten Commandments have the concept of loyalty in common. Here God commands that we do nothing to interfere with the loyalty of those who are in relationships with others.

In the afterword, God states that those who are loyal to God and show it through the keeping of these Commandments will receive steadfast love from God. God's determination that the Commandments be kept, however, is based upon the good that God intends for all people. Each of the Ten Commandments preserves relationships with God and with our neighbors.

WARM-UP Invite the group to think about television advertising. Can they think of any products that try to get them to be disloyal to one product and loyal to the product they offer? Do they think those products have anything to do with a their relationship to God and with others?

ACTIVITY Read aloud the Tenth Commandment and Luther's explanation of it as well as the afterward and Luther's explanation of it on pages 21 and 22 of *A Contemporary Translation of Luther's Small Catechism*.

Then, instruct them to work in pairs. Each pair is to make a list of at least five kinds of relationships that require loyalty and the limits to loyalty that is expected. Then gather the pairs together and have each pair share its list as you write the ideas on the chalkboard or chart paper. Ask them how people can be loyal and yet maintain their individual responsibilities.

Remind the group that in their study of the other nine commandments, they have seen that each commandment is there to benefit people in some way. Ask the class why they think God included this commandment warning us not to damage the loyalty in relationships.

RESPONSE Ask if there is one commandment that is more important than the others. Have them listen to what Jesus said when some Pharisees asked that same question. Read aloud Matthew 22:34-40 and then ask these questions.

1. How did Jesus answer the Pharisees' question?

2. What is the key idea that Jesus says is behind all of the Ten Commandments?

3. What do you think of Jesus' answer?

Apostles' Creed
Three in One

FOCUS   The Apostles' Creed tells us about the one God who reveals himself as Father, Son, and Holy Spirit.

BACKGROUND   The Apostles' Creed goes back to the very beginnings of the Christian church. Though it probably did not originate with the twelve apostles, a creed similar to the one we now have was being used by the church in the year 200. For hundreds of years, the Apostle's Creed has served as a boundary marker for what the church may and may not say about God as Father, Son, and Holy Spirit.

The church is continually tempted by false teaching. For example, in our time there are many who say that Jesus was a great man and perhaps a prophet, but they stop short of saying he was divine. However, if Jesus was not God, how can we be saved? The Apostles' Creed provides a check against such errors because it tells us that the very essence of God was present in Jesus.

It should also be noted that the purpose of the Creed in the catechism is not to provide an exhaustive explanation of God and the mystery of the Trinity. Luther's explanations make clear that he was trying to show how God intersects in a personal and powerful way in the life of the believer. The Creed is not something merely to be *believed*.

Luther wanted the Creed not only to penetrate our minds but also our hearts and souls. He wanted us to be captivated, even overwhelmed, by the kind of God who has claimed us as his children.

WARM-UP   Read the Creed together in various ways. It is on page 23 of *A Contemporary Translation of Luther's Small Catechism*. Ask if there are words that need explanation. Try whispering it together, shouting it, and reading it in a round.

ACTIVITY   Write these questions on separate note cards. Divide everyone into four groups. Assign each group one question to discuss. Ask each group to prepare to teach the question and the answer to the group in the best possi-

ble way in a short amount of time. When everyone is ready, let the groups begin to teach. Answers follow.

1. What are the three parts of the Apostles' Creed? *(Beliefs about God: Father, Son, and Holy Spirit.)*

2. Why is the Creed important? *(It introduces us to God and gives us words to talk about the Holy Spirit.)*

3. What else do we need to do besides believe the Creed? *(God wants us to KNOW things about GOD, and also LIVE accordingly.)*

4. Imagine that a non-Christian approached you in school and accused you of worshiping three Gods. How would you respond? *(Christians worship one God who has revealed himself in three persons. The God who made us, loves us, and stays with us.)*

RESPONSE   Provide various hats, and invite everyone to wear a hat. Begin a discussion about how a hat tells us something about the identity of the person wearing it. *(For example, a cowboy hat tells us something about what a cowboy does. The wide brim protects the wearer from sun and rain, and the hat can be used as a pillow at night.)*

To help people reflect on the Trinity, think about God wearing different hats. Have some fun with this.

◆ Make a crown that weaves together some type of greenery to talk about God as ruler and creator (see Psalm 139:13-15).

◆ Make a crown of thorns from wire and nails to talk about God as Savior (see Mark 15:16-20).

◆ Make a hat that symbolizes fire to talk about the Holy Spirit and how God purifies and sanctifies us (see Acts 2).

Let group members take the initiative in making connections with the hats and some of the ways God acts among us.

See corresponding activity in the *Youth Journal*, page 43.

Apostles' Creed
God the Creator

FOCUS God has created me and everything that exists.

 BACKGROUND In the explanation of the First Article of the Creed, the Small Catechism says that "God has created me together with all creatures." Luther's intent is to underline that all of life is a gift of God. Nature is not merely the result of random forces; it bears the stamp and guidance of a creator. Nor should humans be too quick to boast of their talents and achievements. All that we have and do is by the will of God.

Luther was also well aware that when we talk of creation, our language tends to become abstract, as if God were distant and remote. He took great pains to emphasize that you and I are personal recipients of the gifts flowing from God's gracious hand. Notice how that little word *me* appears again and again in the explanation the First Article: God has created *me*, God has given *me*, God protects *me* . . . and preserves *me*. This is not a God who is removed and aloof. This is a creator who is also a Father, a God who is intimately involved in my life.

For the most part, we take the basic necessities of life for granted. When was the last time we really stopped and pondered the miracle contained in every loaf of bread or the marvelous way the human body and mind are constructed? In this article, Luther hopes we will open our eyes and see the wonders within and around us as evidence of God's providential and fatherly care.

WARM-UP Break into two groups. In one minute, see which group can compile the longest list of things that God has created.

ACTIVITY Distribute scissors, old magazines, large sheets of paper, glue, and a photograph of each student. Turn to Genesis 1 in the Bible and assign each person (or small group) one day in the creation story. Have each person/ group make a collage from the magazines that identifies God's actions on that day. (Creativity will be needed on day seven!) Be sure that this phrase is found at the bottom of each collage: AND GOD SAW THAT IT WAS GOOD.

For the day six collage, use pictures of all group members. (If you lack photographs, group members could draw their own pictures.)

RESPONSE Read together the First Article of the Creed and Luther's explanation of it on page 25 of *A Contemporary Translation of Luther's Small Catechism*. Discuss the following questions.

1. What does it mean to say that God is creator and Father? *(God not only creates; God also watches over creation.)*

2. Do we really "own" anything? Why or why not? *(No, strictly speaking, for God is the owner of everything. We are simply the caretakers of God's creation.)*

3. If you are "created good," what difference does that make for your life? *(It means I am special to God, and so I can feel good about myself and realize that others are special to God, too.)*

 See corresponding activity in the *Youth Journal*, page 44.

Apostles' Creed
To the Rescue

FOCUS   Jesus came to rescue us from sin.

BACKGROUND   If the Apostles' Creed is likened to a song, Luther really turns up the volume in the Second Article. He can scarcely contain his delight as he describes what God has done for us in Jesus Christ. But before we can focus on that joy, we must first recognize our deep need for Christ. In his explanation, Luther makes clear that at great cost Jesus "redeemed me, a lost and condemned human being."

It is that last phrase that makes us wince. We resist with every fiber of our being admitting that we are "lost and condemned." We prefer to think that we can manage just fine on our own, without any help from God. Early in his life, Luther believed he could conquer this dark power by his own good works. But his attempt to do this nearly drove him mad. No sooner did he think he had transformed himself into a "good" person, when a voice would rear up in back of his head and remind him of a sin he had committed.

Luther's experience is universal. It is vital to recognize that an old Adam/Eve lurks within us, wanting desperately to be in charge and take control. This does not mean that we are created bad. We learned in the First Article that we are part of God's good creation. But, we are afflicted with a grave disease and are in urgent need of a physician who can restore us to health. We need someone who can return us to the people God meant us to be. As we come to confess the depth of our sin, we open up to the whole new world God has waiting for us in Christ. But that is already looking ahead to the next session.

WARM-UP   Have the group compile a sin list. Write these sins on the chalkboard or chart paper as they are named.

ACTIVITY   Read together the Second Article of the Creed and Luther's explanation of it on page 27 of *A Contemporary Translation of Luther's Small Catechism*. Give each person two differently colored pieces of construction paper. Provide a bright light, chalk, scissors, tape, and glue. It may sound strange, but each of us is two people. There is the old Adam/Eve and there is the new creation we have become in Christ. To illustrate this, have someone sit in a chair in between a bright light and a space on a wall or chalkboard. Tape one paper to the wall and use the chalk to trace the person's silhouette. Make a copy of the silhouette on the other paper and glue the two halves together. On one silhouette, have the person make some sort of mark or symbol to represent two sins that have been committed. Leave the other paper unmarked to symbolize our new life in Christ.

RESPONSE   Divide everyone into small groups to discuss the following questions. Review their responses when everyone is finished. The answers follow.

1. What is sin? *(Sin happens when we put our trust in things God has made—money, clothes, sports—and not God.)*

2. Read Psalm 51:1-4 and talk about the sin that clings to each one of us. Why is it important to recognize our sin? *(See Luke 18:9-14; so we don't become proud and fail to see our need for Christ.)*

3. Why is it hard to admit we are sinners? *(The old Adam/Eve wants to be in charge.)*

4. What happens when we don't admit our sin? *(Our conscience accuses us and makes us feel badly.)*

   See corresponding activity in the *Youth Journal*, page 45.

Apostles' Creed
Jesus Saves

FOCUS   On the cross Jesus takes our sin upon himself and gives us his righteousness, innocence, and peace.

 BACKGROUND   Luther's goal was to make people realize that Christ had truly done something about their own sin. Luther liked to speak of Christ's relationship to our sin in terms of something he called the "joyous exchange." On the cross, Jesus had taken upon himself all the sins of the world. Luther even called Jesus the "greatest sinner"—not because of his own sin (Christ in his own person was sinless) but because Jesus bore bodily every actual sin ever committed. The logic is breathtaking. Because our sins are now on Christ, we no longer have them. Therefore, we are free from sin and also given Christ's righteousness and purity.

Luther would sometimes explain this in terms of a marriage. When two people wed, what was the husband's (including the unpaid bills and suspect reputation) now becomes the wife's and vice versa. So it is with Christ and us. Faith can be likened to the wedding. In our "marriage" with Christ we receive his innocence and blessedness. And in return, Christ gets the soiled garments of his bride—our lusts, dishonesty, and greed. It all sounds terribly unfair, but then that is the kind of God we have.

WARM-UP   Have the group list on the chalkboard or chart paper as many different names of Jesus that come to mind. (*Christ, Lord, Savior, Son of God, Son of Man, Messiah, Lamb of God, and so forth.*)

ACTIVITY   Display a cross that is large enough to support clothing. Provide markers, old shirts (brought by group members), and enough white robes (choir robes will work nice-

ly) or white shirts for each class member to have one. Darken the room to candlelight.

Read together 2 Corinthians 5:16-21. Tell the group that the old shirts stand for the "old" life—life outside of Christ. In silence, have the group tear and stain the old shirts, with each tear and stain representing a sin they regret. Have individuals come forward, one by one, to the cross you have draped in white garments. Tell them to leave their old shirts on the cross and give them white garments to put on, symbolizing the righteousness of Christ. Each time a soiled shirt is exchanged for a white garment, read 2 Corinthians 5:21 out loud.

RESPONSE   Read together the Second Article of the Creed and Luther's explanation of it on page 27 of *A Contemporary Translation of Luther's Small Catechism*. Write these questions on chalkboard or chart paper on various sides of the room. Encourage people to write their answers under the questions. When everyone is done, review their responses.

1. Why is Jesus' death on the cross like a great exchange? (*Christ Jesus receives our sin, while we receive his righteousness.*)

2. How could Martin Luther call Jesus the "greatest sinner of all?" (*Because Jesus took upon himself the sin of the entire world.*)

3. What difference does the cross make in your daily life? (*Knowing that Jesus loves me so much so as to die for me, it is no longer necessary to prove my worth to others.*)

4. What problem might surface when the cross is worn as a decoration? (*The cross is much more than jewelry; it is what gives us life, peace, and hope.*)

Apostles' Creed
The Work of the Spirit

FOCUS   The Holy Spirit brings us to faith in Christ.

 BACKGROUND   Luther's explanation to the Third Article of the Creed begins with the astonishing claim: "I believe that by my own understanding or strength I cannot believe in Jesus Christ my Lord or come to him, but instead the Holy Spirit has called me. . . ." Having established in the last article that we are beneficiaries of a wondrous exchange, it might be thought that it is now our responsibility to "claim" Christ as our own. But Luther says that our relationship with Christ is not in our control!

At first the old Adam/Eve within finds this to be threatening. Questions rush to the surface: You mean I can't even decide for Christ? Isn't there something I must do? However, the God who creates and redeems us isn't about to let us go our own way. The third person of the Trinity, the Holy Spirit, creates faith and sustains us in that faith. In other words, the Spirit is the glue that attracts us and keeps us connected to Christ.

The work of the Spirit is wrapped up in the mystery of love. On a human level, we don't decide to fall in love. Rather, it is something in the lover that attracts us. Similarly, Christ comes to us, bestowing his gifts of forgiveness and life. Can we do anything but yield to this greatest lover of all? In our baptism, God in his grace has chosen us as his children. Would we really want it any other way? Isn't it comforting to know in times of temptation, doubt, and darkness that our identity as God's children holds firm in spite of the voices in our head that seem to say otherwise?

WARM-UP   As a group, memorize Ephesians 2:8-9. Focus on the memorization of the message, not the words, in this passage. Use a rap rhythm or a familiar melody to make memorization easier.

ACTIVITY   Read together the Third Article of the Creed as found on page 29 of *A Contemporary Translation of Luther's Small Catechism.* Have group members write a cinquain (5-line poem) on the Holy Spirit. It is not necessary for a cinquain to rhyme.
- The first line is the subject.
- The next line has two words that describe the subject.
- The third line has three words describing an activity of the subject.
- The fourth line has four words describing your feelings about the subject.
- The last line is one word that means the same as the first line.

An example:

> Snow
> White wet
> Gently falling down
> It makes me smile
> Flakes

Have everyone read and sign their cinquains and then make a "cinquain wall" in a public place in the church so adults can read the poems.

RESPONSE   Check for understanding by discussing the following questions, either in small groups or together.

1. What does it mean to say that faith is a gift of the Holy Spirit? *(It means that we cannot take credit for believing in Jesus; it is God's Spirit working in us that allows us to believe.)*

2. Why is this teaching comforting? *(In times of temptation it is important to know that we don't hold onto Christ; rather, he holds onto us.)*

3. What would you say to a friend who told you she had "made a decision for Jesus"? *(Congratulate her and gently explain that it was Jesus who found her and not the other way around.)*

Apostles' Creed
The Fruit of the Spirit

FOCUS   The Holy Spirit creates the church and brings us to eternal life.

 BACKGROUND   We have spoken of how God works through the Holy Spirit to bring us to Christ. The fruit of the Spirit's work is the church. As Luther notes in the Small Catechism, it is the Spirit who "calls, gathers, enlightens and makes holy the whole Christian church on earth." The church is nothing other than those made alive in Christ by the Holy Spirit.

How does the Spirit come to us? Luther taught that the Spirit can come whenever the Bible is read. The Spirit can come when we remember our baptisms or when we receive Christ's body and blood at the Lord's table. The Spirit also works when we gather with fellow Christians and share concerns about our lives, families, and communities.

Because the old Adam/Eve within us is eager to lead us away from Christ, the Holy Spirit is very busy keeping God's children united to him. Those whom the Spirit makes alive in Christ also have the promise of eternal life. Because Jesus has been raised from the dead, those joined to Jesus in their baptism have a resurrection in their future. As Luther puts it in the Small Catechism: "On the last day the Holy Spirit will raise me and all the dead and give me and all believers in Christ an eternal life." God simply refuses to give up on us! Not even death has the final say. Beyond the grave we have a glorious future in heaven with Christ and all the saints.

WARM-UP   Write on the board all the responses the group gives to this question: What happens right after we die?

ACTIVITY   Read together the Third Article of the Creed on page 29 in *A Contemporary Trans-*lation of *Luther's Small Catechism*. Have people write their own obituaries. Share with them a good example from the newspaper or your personal obituary. Provide them with a format that may include the following information: name, date and place of birth, baptism day, education, occupation, residences, family information, hobbies, survivors, church membership, age and cause of death. Encourage everyone to provide a story of his or her life. Avoid the mere collection of facts and dates. Have them keep this information for later in the session.

Break into small groups and discuss the following questions.

1. What is our only hope for eternal life? *(Jesus was raised from the dead.)*

2. Read Romans 8:31-39. Why do you think this passage is often read at funerals? *(Because it says nothing—not even death—can keep us from the love of God.)*

3. Why does the Creed talk about the resurrection of the body? *(The Creed does not separate the body from the spirit; our bodies, as God's good creation, will be raised in a new and glorious form.)*

4. What happens to someone who commits suicide? *(If the person believes in Christ, he or she will share in his resurrection, just like all believers.)*

RESPONSE   Give the group members time to review the obituaries they have written for themselves. Encourage them to identify themselves as children of God, followers of Jesus Christ. Then take time to share them and post them.

Lord's Prayer

First Petition

BACKGROUND   Martin Luther's catechism breaks the Lord's Prayer into seven petitions, or requests, in which we ask God for help in relating to God through faith and in choosing how to live. Luther also included questions and answers about the prayer's introduction and the closing words to help us gain a deeper understanding about the prayer that Jesus taught his first followers.

In this session we will focus on the words from and about the introduction and the First Petition of the Lord's Prayer. They are words in which we turn our whole body, mind, and spirit to God.

◆ These words remind us that God relates with us as a loving parent.

◆ These words also remind us of God's holy name. While God's name is always holy, we pray for God's help in keeping God's name holy in our words and in our actions. Jesus' example shows us how to do this. In Luther's introduction and explanation of the First Petition, he helps us see that we, too, may begin our prayers as did Jesus with praise, glory, and honor to God and God's holy name.

◆ Reproducible Page 9 may be used with each of the sessions on the Lord's Prayer.

WARM-UP   Ask people what they have been taught to do with their bodies when they pray. *(Most may answer that they fold their hands as well as bow their heads.)* While this posture is common for little children so their hands and eyes do not wander during prayer, there is another way to pray. Invite them to open their hands, palms up, with elbows at their sides. Ask them how that feels and what they think that posture may symbolize. *(It may seem strange, unnatural, or even embarrassing to them. Yet, praying with hands relaxed and palms spread out may symbolize a willingness to receive God's help and let go of whatever we see as dirty or spoiled in our lives.)*

Invite the group to read with you the catechism's introduction and the First Petition of the Lord's Prayer and their explanations as found on pages 32 and 33 of *A Contemporary Translation of Luther's Small Catechism*.

ACTIVITY   Give each person a half sheet of paper. Invite them to name something or someone they admire: a school, a professional athlete, a musical group, a singer, or an actor. Tell them to name something or someone that they would be glad to advertise on their T-shirts, sweatshirts, or baseball caps. Have people exchange their papers. Now have each person write some unconstructive criticism (bashing) of the name he or she was given. After everyone has done that, pass the papers back to the owners. Ask the owners to describe how the criticism makes them feel.

This time, have people write "God" or "Jesus" on the back of their papers. Invite them to write down words or phrases that would come to their minds if negative comments were written about God's name.

RESPONSE   Read together the First Petition of the Lord's Prayer on page 33 of *A Contemporary Translation of Luther's Small Catechism*. We feel hurt or angry when people dishonor the name of a school, a person, or our God who is special to us. Invite people to take turns recalling ways they heard or saw someone dishonoring God's name. Also ask them to describe how one person's behavior may influence the words and actions of others. After a moment say, "Now you and I can begin to realize how hard each of us may need to work at keeping God's name holy in our speech and in our actions. Let's use the words from Psalm 57:9 as a prayer that helps us remember how God's people keep God's name holy."

Lord's Prayer
Second Petition

FOCUS We pray to be an ongoing part of God's kingdom, which has come near and which is inevitably coming in its fullness.

 BACKGROUND God's kingdom, which is God's righteous rule, comes without our praying for it. One place we read about the kingdom is in the description of the beginning of Jesus' public ministry as recorded in Mark 1:14-15. That kingdom or rule of God came near when Jesus freed people from whatever was broken in their lives and from whatever kept them addicted or in bondage. The total rule of God continues to come as the Holy Spirit guides us into deeper faith and godly living. We also believe God's kingdom will surely come. We pray in this petition that we may be part of that freeing, righteous rule of God.

- Reproducible Page 9 may be used with each of the sessions on the Lord's Prayer.

WARM-UP Begin by reading together the Second Petition and its explanation on page 34 of *A Contemporary Translation of Luther's Small Catechism*. Then say, "It's time for a parade."

- Ask the group to suggest some people who are likely to be in a parade.
- Also have them describe some people who may be watching a parade.
- Have them imagine what it would be like to attend a parade if you could not see.
- Who do they think enjoys a parade more—the participants or the people watching the parade?

ACTIVITY Invite people to open their Bibles to Luke 18:35-43. Read the story about Jesus and the blind man near Jericho. Ask them to imagine themselves as the blind person along the "parade" route of Jesus. Then have them respond to the following questions as if *they* were the blind person alongside the road near Jericho.

1. What are they feeling and thinking as they *hear* the following?
- a crowd passing;
- Jesus of Nazareth passing by;

- their own voices shouting "Jesus, Son of David, have mercy on me!";
- Jesus' ordering persons to bring them to him;
- the voice of Jesus asking what they want him to do for them;
- themselves pleading "Lord, let me see again";
- Jesus declaring "Receive your sight; your faith has saved you!"

2. What are they thinking and feeling as they *do* the following?
- regain their sight;
- follow Jesus;
- glorify God;
- hear the crowd around them praising God.

RESPONSE Prior to the session, put water in the baptismal font in your congregation's worship space. Take the group there. Tell everyone that God's rule broke into the world of the blind man at Jericho, as well as at the tomb on Easter morning. In those places and elsewhere, the public outpouring of the Holy Spirit upon the early followers of Jesus on Pentecost during and following the earthly life of Jesus made it possible for the people to be delivered from the lasting power of evil.

That same powerful rule of God broke into the young people's world beginning with their baptism. Invite them to dip their fingers in the water of the baptismal font and trace the sign of the cross on their foreheads, saying "I have been baptized." If time permits, urge them to look around the worship space to see other symbols of the presence of God's kingdom. *(The cross, banner, picture, and so forth.)*

In the Second Petition of the Lord's Prayer, we pray that God will continue to break into our lives through the sending of the Holy Spirit. With that gift we can believe this good news. We can praise God with our lips and with our lives.

 See corresponding activity in the *Youth Journal*, page 46.

Lord's Prayer
Third Petition

FOCUS We pray God to continually unleash God's power to defeat the evil forces in and around us that vigorously oppose the will of God and attempt to weaken our faith in God.

BACKGROUND Some people will ask a family member, friend, or their pastor to "say a little prayer" for them when they have to go to the hospital for surgery, apply for a new job, or take an important test. The Third Petition reminds us how important it is to say the really big prayers.

◆ Big prayers sometimes involve struggling with following God's will, the way Jesus struggled in prayer in the Garden of Gethsemane (Luke 22:39-46).

◆ Big prayers sometimes involve praying for solid confidence in God and for a strong faith- the kind of faith we need for every day.

There is good news. God hears our big prayers. God gives us the very power of God to do and say that which is pleasing in God's sight.

◆ Reproducible Page 9 may be used with each of the sessions on the Lord's Prayer.

◆ Reproducible Page 10 may be used with the Third Petition.

WARM-UP Read together the Third Petition and its explanation on page 35 of *A Contemporary Translation of Luther's Small Catechism.* Have the group read or sing the words to Martin Luther's hymn "A Mighty Fortress Is Our God" (*LBW* 229). This hymn is also on page 79 of *A Contemporary Translation of Luther's Small Catechism.* The second stanza of this Reformation hymn declares that God has sent Jesus to be present with us to be victorious over evil. The third stanza says "hordes of devils fill the land." Ask the group to say that phrase, in unison, three times. Tell them they will look for examples of this phrase later in the session.

ACTIVITY Designate one area of the room as "DOING GOD'S WILL," another area as "NOT DOING GOD'S WILL," and the area in between as "NOT SURE." *As you read the following, have the group stand and move to the area of the*

room they think is being described in each of the following vignettes.

1. Imagine it's your first day in a new school. Suddenly, an older student purposely knocks some books out of your hand. *Move to the area of the room that describes what that older student just did.*

2. You go to your assigned room. It is filled with people whose last names are from the same part of the alphabet as yours. You find yourself separated from the only friend you have in the class. A student next to you whom you have never seen before says hello and tells you her name. Then she begins telling you some funny things that happened to her, and you laugh. *Move to the area of the room that describes what you are doing.*

3. Thankfully, you and your friend share the same lunch period. You sit next to each other after getting your food. When you leave the table to get a napkin and your friend turns to talk with someone across the aisle, another student dumps loads of pepper all over your food. *Move to the area of the room that describes the stranger's actions.*

4. Thoughts of using God's name to curse that stranger fly into your head. *Move to the area of the room that describes your feelings.*

5. After a flash of anger sweeps over you, the words "God help me to be forgiving" come into your mind. *Move to the area of the room that describes your attitude.*

Note that following God's will means paying attention to things that are happening around you and putting God's will before your own.

RESPONSE Bring newspapers into the room. Ask half the group to find stories about people who are living in ways that oppose God's will. Find out if the situations in the articles are examples of places where "hordes of devils fill the land." Ask the others to write three or four sentences about someone they know who does God's will.

Remind them that wherever the good news of God's love goes, that good news meets opposition. The newspaper stories will point out how some people oppose God's will. Thanks be to God we can work for change and ask God to defeat any evil that would tempt us to weaken our resolve to be faithful witnesses to God's love.

Lord's Prayer
Fourth Petition

FOCUS   We pray to God for a genuine spirit of thankfulness as we receive God's gifts to meet all our daily needs.

BACKGROUND   In the first three petitions of the Lord's Prayer, we pray for God. That may be a surprise to us. We pray for God's name to be kept holy among us; for God's kingdom to come among us; and for God's will to be done among us.

Now we begin to pray the word *give*. Another possible surprise is the way in which we use the word *give* in the Fourth Petition. We are not asking God to give us all we need for daily living. God does that out of God's grace. Rather, we pray for another gift. We pray for the gift of a constantly thankful heart, as God gives us daily living needs.

◆ Reproducible Page 9 may be used with each of the sessions on the Lord's Prayer.

WARM-UP   Prior to this session, bake some bread in the oven at church or prepare some pizza or popcorn in a microwave oven there. Let people take a strong smell of the food you have prepared. (You may wish to let them eat some of this food while you relate the following information.)

Tell them about the walk-in food pantries that were common when many of their grandparents were young. As a person stepped into the food pantry, which was built alongside the kitchen, that person could see and smell the food on the shelves or cooling on the counter. An abundance of food surrounded the person. Invite the students to picture such a walk-in food pantry with its sights and sounds. Ask them if it would be easy to pray in such a place for the gift of food.

Then tell them that when Jesus commanded his followers to go into their rooms and "shut the door and pray" (Matthew 6:6), the word he used for *room* literally meant a storeroom or food pantry. What an ideal place to pray! What

a place to give thanks for the food and all the gifts which surround us every day.

ACTIVITY   Read together the Fourth Petition of the Lord's Prayer and its explanation on page 36 of *A Contemporary Translation of Luther's Small Catechism*. Provide tape, one old magazine or four or five magazine pages, and scissors for each student. Tape a long sheet of newsprint or computer paper on the chalkboard or wall.

Ask them to look at the magazine pages and look for pictures of things they need for daily living. Tighten the focus of this activity by having them focus on things that they take for granted. Have them cut out those pictures and make a collage with them on the paper you have displayed. Make this activity a continuous prayer by asking each person to say "Thank you God for . . ." as his or her picture(s) is added to the collage. Conclude this prayer by saying, "God help us not to take these gifts for granted."

RESPONSE   Some nations have one day set apart each year as Thanksgiving Day. The Fourth Petition of the Lord's Prayer encourages us to give thanks daily for the gift of each day and all the basic needs we receive. This petition urges us to adopt the attitude of "thanks-living."

Have someone read aloud the story of the 10 lepers in Luke 17:11-19. Ask how the story of the 10 lepers brings to life the words of the meaning of the Fourth Petition. *(God gives daily bread to all people; we ask that God will help us to receive our daily bread with thanks.)*

   See corresponding activity in the *Youth Journal*, page 47.

Lord's Prayer
Fifth Petition

FOCUS   We pray God's forgiveness of our sins will motivate us to eagerly forgive those who hurt us.

 BACKGROUND   We know from our experiences that when someone holds grudges against another person and refuses to forgive him or her, that person often refuses to listen or talk to the person. That is why we pray in this petition for God's gracious forgiveness. We sense that without our being forgiven and restored to a right relationship with God, our prayers may not be heard. We also pray God to use our gratitude over being forgiven to make us forgiving persons. We, the *forgiven*, pray to *be* forgiving.

◆ Reproducible Page 9 may be used with each of the sessions on the Lord's Prayer.

WARM-UP   Speak the following statement with teeth clenched and with anger in your voice. **"How could you do that to me? I hate you for that! Get out of here! I never want to see you again."** Ask people to suggest what the result of this statement might be. *(It suggests a permanently broken relationship, and continued anger and hurt. The statement will be remembered, together with the pain that it caused and continues to cause.)*

ACTIVITY   Read together the Fifth Petition and its explanation on page 37 of *A Contemporary Translation of Luther's Small Catechism*. Invite people to turn to the marriage service on pages 61-65 of *A Contemporary Translation of Luther's Small Catechism*. Quickly point out the different parts of the service, beginning on page 63. Find out how many people have ever attended a wedding. Ask what one word occurs many times in a wedding service? *(They may suggest the words "love," "commitment," and "promise.")* Ask if they remember the bride and groom saying vows to each other. Tell them that the vows, or promises, that the bride and groom make before the altar of God and the gathered people are a very special part of the marriage service.

Write on the chalkboard or chart paper the following sentence: "I will forgive you as we have been forgiven." This sentence is a part of one of the promises or vows that some Christian couples choose to say to each other during their wedding service. Invite group members to turn their heads or chairs toward the persons next to them and work in pairs. Give them several minutes to discuss why the words on the chalkboard or chart paper are important promises to make at a wedding. It may help them if they think of specific family situations where husbands and wives need to be able to forgive one another.

Ask for volunteers to share some of their responses. While they are in pairs, ask them to discuss if they think it easier for a couple to forgive each other if they both are Christians or if one or neither the bride or groom are Christian. *(Answers will vary.)*

RESPONSE   Give everyone a piece of paper and a pencil. Invite them to copy down this brief prayer: **"Give us courage, dear God, to forgive all who have injured us as we have been forgiven by you. Amen."**

Now have them think privately of a person who is particularly difficult for them to forgive. Then ask them to describe the TYPES of people that have come to mind, naming only the very general characteristics of that person's personality or behavior and NOT the person's name. Make a list of those characteristics on the chalkboard or chart paper. Then ask the students to look at the list and see if they have ever been guilty of any of the characteristics that have made others seem unforgivable to them. After a moment or two, ask the participants to look again at the brief prayer above and then pray it with you.

Lord's Prayer
Sixth Petition

FOCUS We pray to God that when we are severely tested by trials or temptations, our faith and loyalty are not taken from us.

 BACKGROUND We pray "Save us from the time of trial." By praying this petition we acknowledge there will be times of trial, temptation, and testing in our lives. The power of evil, the lure of doing things that we know displease God, and media's constant encouragement to reward ourselves with instant gratification—all of these things are real.

In explaining the meaning of the Sixth Petition, Martin Luther says that the devil, the world, and our flesh try to deceive us and draw us away from firm faith in God. That is why we need to ask God to help us when such times of testing occur. With God's strong help and guidance we can remain firm in our faith and refuse to submit to the forces of evil.

♦ Reproducible Page 9 may be used with each of the sessions on the Lord's Prayer.

WARM-UP Tell the group this old adage: **"The devil trembles when he sees / the Christian person on the knee."** Remind the group that one posture for prayer is to be on one's knees. This old saying suggests that the devil trembles when the Christian is seen in prayer. In what ways might this saying be true?

ACTIVITY Assign individuals these roles to pantomime when they hear something about them read: Peter, first servant girl, second servant girl, silent bystanders, and speaking bystander. Now read them Matthew 26:69-75, the account of Peter's denial of Jesus, Establish the scene in the students' minds before you begin: Peter may be slipping through the shadows way behind the procession that is leading Jesus to be tried. Even when Peter thinks he is far enough away from Jesus, someone confronts him. Help them sense how Peter was also on trial while Jesus was being tried at the home of the high priest.

Read together the Sixth Petition and its explanation on page 38 of *A Contemporary Translation of Luther's Small Catechism.*

Invite everyone to gather in groups of three or four. Have each group choose one of the following situations to discuss. Have them identify ways that the persons involved in these situations are having their faith and loyalty to God tested.

1. It's state tournament time. You have gone with your parents to the city where your older brother or sister's high school team is participating in the tournament. You meet several of your friends and their families at a shopping mall. Your parents say it is all right for you to spend some time with them. Almost immediately, one of them suggests you go into a store and see if you can shoplift something without getting caught.

2. In the locker room at school someone is passing around a magazine with pictures of naked people. The person urges you to "feast your eyes" on one of the pictures. You indicate you're not interested. The person asks, "What's the matter with you?"

RESPONSE Distribute copies of *Lutheran Book of Worship.* Have everyone turn to page 198. Point out the Affirmation of Baptism service. Ask them the questions in rubric 12 (pp. 199-200). Invite them to respond, "I do." Also ask them the questions before they repeat each of the three sections of the Apostles' Creed. Point out that it may be easier to make this confession in worship than it is to live out the meaning of those words in their daily lives. Now invite the group to read the Sixth Petition and its explanation in unison.

 See corresponding activity in the *Youth Journal*, page 48.

Lord's Prayer
Seventh Petition

We pray in this summary petition that God will deliver us from all evils, bodily and spiritually.

BACKGROUND The newspaper headlines and television newscasts reveal the constant onslaught of evil. War, greed, revenge, hunger, and disease are only a few examples of such evil in our world and lives. That is why we take the following words from 1 Peter 5:8 to heart.

We know the devil can be sly and cunning, gently trying to lure us away from our faith in God by constantly questioning God's Word and intent, just like the serpent did in the Garden of Eden. Thanks be to God we also know the stronger, more trustworthy voice of Jesus who declares, "In the world you face persecution. But take courage; I have conquered the world!" (John 16:33b). Jesus promised, "Remember: I am with you always, to the end of the age" (Matthew 28:20b) and "I will come again and will take you to myself, so that where I am, there you may be also" (John 14:3b).

◆ Reproducible Page 9 may be used with each of the sessions on the Lord's Prayer.

WARM-UP Inform the group that in any given year there are thousands of missing youth. Ninety-nine percent of those young people are runaways. Ask the group to explain why so many young people run away from home. Record their answers on the chalkboard or chart paper. Invite people to suggest dangers that runaway youth may face.

ACTIVITY Invite everyone to follow along as you read them the Seventh Petition and Luth-er's explanation of it on page 39 of *A Contemporary Translation of Luther's Small Catechism*. Find out if they know about the phone number 911—the emergency help line. Tell them that they may work individually or in small groups on this activity. Distribute lined paper and pencils and ask them to turn their papers horizontally. On the top left side, have them write "911" and on the top right side "God." Have them draw a vertical line down the middle of the paper. Under the number 911, have them list examples of situations that might cause people to call this number for help for themselves or someone else. Under the heading "God," have them list examples of situations that might cause people to call on God in prayer for themselves or someone else.

RESPONSE Ask the group if they feel calling 911 is more or less assuring than calling to God in prayer. Be sure to remind them that when we conclude our prayers with the word *Amen*, we say that word with confidence, like we are putting a gigantic exclamation point at the end of what we have said. We have prayed with complete confidence that God has heard us. So we firmly say *Amen*, believing that *it shall be so*. We confidently follow the words of James 1:5-6. Read the passage to them. Then invite the group to read aloud together the conclusion and Luther's explanation of it on page 40 of *A Contemporary Translation of Luther's Small Catechism*.

Sacraments: Baptism and Holy Communion

Rescued!

FOCUS   In Baptism God rescues us from everything that threatens us and gives us new life in Christ.

 BACKGROUND   Nothing that happens to us is more significant than Baptism. Baptism is truly God's "rescue operation" in our lives. When we are baptized, God frees us from all that endangers us and gives us a future with God forever. It is our immersion—perhaps literally—into all that Christ has done to save us. Baptism is also our welcome into the church—the community of all persons who have been so rescued.

WARM-UP   Prior to the group session find drawings, photos, and newspaper headlines about water. Post these around the room. Also, make a Graffiti Wall by taping a large sheet of chart paper to one wall of the room. In large, bold letters print on it the phrase: "WATER, WATER, EVERYWHERE." Give everyone markers, and invite them to go to the Graffiti Wall and spend several minutes making words, symbols, drawings of all sorts of ways that water is used in the world.

After all have had a chance to add at least one thing to the Graffiti Wall, ask them to identify:
◆ ways that water can be dangerous, and
◆ ways that water is life-giving.

ACTIVITY   Ask the group to think of a time when they or someone they know was rescued from danger. Invite several to share their stories. Tell the group that in this session they will learn about the greatest "rescue operation" a person can ever experience: Holy Baptism.

Invite group members to turn to "The Sacrament of Holy Baptism" beginning on page 41 of *A Contemporary Translation of Luther's Small Catechism*. Ask them to follow along while you read aloud the first two sections: "What is Baptism?" and "What gifts or benefits does Baptism grant?"

Write these words on the chalkboard or chart paper: SIN, DEATH, DEVIL. Ask class members to close their eyes as you slowly repeat these words several times. Then ask them to open their eyes and share the images or ideas that came to them as they heard these words. Jot down their responses behind each word.

Then ask the group: What is threatening or dangerous about sin? About death? About the devil? Again, record their responses on the chalkboard behind each word.

Conclude this activity by asking: What has God done about sin, death, and the devil? Invite group members to read aloud together the response to the question from the catechism: "What gifts or benefits does Baptism grant?"

RESPONSE   Divide the class into groups of three. Ask each group to create a baptism cheer. Tell them that their cheers should reflect what the group has learned today about baptism as well as how they feel about being baptized children of God. When everyone is ready, give each group a chance to perform its cheer for the class.

See corresponding activity in the *Youth Journal*, page 49.

Sacraments: Baptism and Holy Communion
The Washing Word

FOCUS The rescuing power of Baptism is the Word of God that accompanies the water.

 BACKGROUND Baptism combines an ordinary earthly substance (water) with an extraordinary out-of-this-world promise (the Word). Both the water and the Word are essential. The water visibly and tangibly links Baptism with all the other ways water is life-giving for us as creatures. But the water isn't the main thing in Baptism. The powerhouse in this sacrament is the Word of God. In Baptism we are given God's triune name: Father, Son, and Holy Spirit. This name grants us access to God and to all God's good gifts—forever!

WARM-UP If possible, hold this session in the worship area of your church building, around the baptismal font. (Before the session make sure that there is water in the font.) If you can't meet in the worship space, place a large bowl of water in your classroom.

Have members of the group stand in a circle around the font and tell how they received their names. Ask: Were you named after someone else? Does your name have a special meaning?

Then, stand by the font and tell the class that in Holy Baptism they received the greatest name of all: God's name. Dip your finger in the water, trace the sign of the cross on each class member's forehead, saying, "In Baptism you were joined to God—the Father, Son, and Holy Spirit."

ACTIVITY Divide into groups of three, and give each group a sheet of chart paper and a marker. Ask the groups to brainstorm a list of ways for one person to communicate to another person the following statement: YOU ARE IMPORTANT TO ME. Encourage the groups to

think of ways to communicate that involve all five senses: seeing, hearing, touching, tasting, smelling.

Give each group an opportunity to share their list with the others. Then ask: Is a message more effective if it appeals to one sense or more than one sense? *(More than one sense.)* Invite someone to read aloud "How can water do such great things?" It is the third section of the discussion of Holy Baptism on page 42 of *A Contemporary Translation of Luther's Small Catechism.*

Point out how in Baptism God uses three of our senses to get through to us—sight, touch and hearing. Ask, "According to this part of the catechism, which sense seems to be most important?" *(Hearing the Word of God that goes along with the water in Baptism is most important.)*

Have the group read aloud together Isaiah 55:10-11. Ask, "What is the most important thing these verses tell us about God's Word?" *(Answers may vary. Some answers may include: it has a power of its own; it does what it says; it accomplishes God's purposes.)*

RESPONSE Write the following unfinished statements on the chalkboard or chart paper:

1. One new thing I learned about Baptism today is . . .
2. Something that still puzzles me about Baptism is . . .
3. Baptism makes my daily life better by . . .

Have everyone sit in a circle and toss a soft object (ball of yarn, nerf ball, or bean bag) around the circle. Tell them that whenever a person catches the object, he/she is to complete one of the statements. Continue until everyone has responded at least once.

Sacraments: Baptism and Holy Communion
Living in Rhythm

FOCUS Baptism moves us into a lifelong rhythm of daily repentance and forgiveness.

BACKGROUND Viewing Baptism as a "once upon a time" event in the past is one of the most common ways this sacrament is misunderstood. In direct response to such a misconception, Martin Luther declared, "In Baptism, every Christian has enough to study and to practice all his life. . . . Thus a Christian life is nothing else than a daily Baptism, once begun and ever continued."[1]

The drowning and rising actions at the heart of the baptismal rite are repeated in the daily practice of confessing sin and receiving forgiveness. Through this rhythm of repentance, believers return to their Baptism and are born again, and again, and again.

WARM-UP When the group members have gathered, ask them to join you in doing some simple exercises—stretching, toe touching, or neck rolls. (Keep the exercises simple, especially if some class members have physical limitations.) Have people name some of the exercises they do every day to keep in shape. Ask: Why is daily exercise necessary for good health?

ACTIVITY Make copies of Reproducible Page 7. Distribute the Bible study sheets on Luke 19:1-10. Divide the class into small groups, and ask these groups to work on the Bible study.

After the Bible study has been completed, inform the class members that the story of Zacchaeus is a wonderful illustration of repentance—and repentance is the key word in this session's encounter with the Small Catechism.

Have them read the fourth section under "The Sacrament of Holy Baptism" on page 43 of

A Contemporary Translation of Luther's Small Catechism. It begins, "What then is the significance of such a baptism with water?" Invite responses to the question "How does the exercise of daily repentance make us stronger and healthier, as baptized children of God?"

RESPONSE Read the following statements and ask group members to position themselves along an imaginary line between two points in the room. Tell them one end of the line represents "AGREE," and the other end represents "DISAGREE." For each statement, invite group members to tell why they are standing in a particular spot along the line.

1. Only holy water that has been specially blessed should be used in Baptism.

2. If a baptized person turns away from God, God also turns away from that person.

3. Baptism is like giving someone a hug and telling them you love them.

4. Since babies don't know what is happening to them, they shouldn't be baptized until they're older.

5. Baptism makes a big difference in how Christians live each day.

6. Since God is the one who acts in Baptism, it would be possible to turn non-believers into Christians simply by sprinkling baptismal water on them.

7. If you are baptized it doesn't matter how you choose to live your life.

8. Babies who die before being baptized can't receive God's love and forgiveness.

---

1. From *What Does This Mean? Luther's Catechisms Today* edited by Phillip E. Pederson, copyright © 1979 Augsburg Publishing House.

Sacraments: Baptism and Holy Communion
Health Food

FOCUS Holy Communion is a real meal that fills us with Christ and nourishes our faith.

 BACKGROUND God never leaves a job unfinished. What God begins in Baptism, God sustains in Holy Communion. In obedience to Christ's loving command, we regularly eat bread and drink wine the way the disciples did the night before Jesus was crucified. In Holy Communion, Christ himself comes to us to renew us in faith. Holy Communion is the original "health food." When we go to the Supper, we are refreshed through the healing power of this gift of life.

WARM-UP Prepare a healthy, tasty snack for everyone to share as they gather. Serve the food from a common plate or bowl. As people enjoy their snack, give them each a large sheet of construction paper and a marker. Ask them to divide the paper into four sections and draw pictures that describe the following:
- their favorite junk food for watching TV;
- the way the table looked at their last big family gathering, including the people who were there;
- their favorite fast food restaurant;
- the healthiest food they like to eat.

Invite class members to display their completed pictures around the class area for all to see.

ACTIVITY Prior to the session, find a copy of Leonardo da Vinci's famous portrait of "The Last Supper." Hold the picture up and ask the group members to tell you everything they know about the picture and the scene it depicts. You might ask:
- Who are all the people in the picture?
- When does this scene take place?
- What might each person around the table be feeling?
- Why is this picture found in so many churches and homes?

Tell the group that Holy Communion has a crucial connection to the Last Supper, and ask them to turn to page 49 of *A Contemporary Translation of Luther's Small Catechism.* Have them read aloud together the first section, "What is the Sacrament of the Altar?" and "Where is this written?"

Divide into groups of two or three people and give each group a note card with one of the following passages written on it: Matthew 9:10-13; Matthew 14:13-21; Luke 24:13-35 (especially verses 30-31); John 12:1-8; and John 21:9-14. Ask each group to describe what happens in their passage, and how people react or respond to Jesus' actions in these meals.

Now have them look once again at the question and response to "What is the Sacrament of the Altar?" Ask them: What is *ordinary* about Holy Communion? *(Bread and wine, eating and drinking.)* What is *extraordinary* about Holy Communion? *(The body and blood of Christ, instituted by Christ.)*

RESPONSE Use a tape recorder or a video camcorder to do some brief "Person on the Street" interviews with the young people. (This could be done while they are doing small group work on previous activities.) Pose questions like: What's one new thing you've learned about Holy Communion today? Why do you go to Holy Communion? What questions do you still have about Holy Communion? When everyone has been interviewed, play the tape for them. Use their responses to fill in any holes in their understanding of this sacrament.

 See corresponding activity in the *Youth Journal*, page 50.

Sacraments: Baptism and Holy Communion
Feast of Freedom

FOCUS In Holy Communion God gives us the most basic necessity of life: the forgiveness of sins.

BACKGROUND Human beings supposedly can survive three minutes without air, three days without water, and three weeks without food. But there's something even more basic to life—the freedom that springs from forgiveness. Without forgiveness, obstacles stand between us and God. Without forgiveness, we have no future with our neighbors. Forgiveness is truly God's "barrier-breaking, future-opening"[1] gift. Forgiveness contains all God's good gifts—for where there is forgiveness of sins, there is also life and salvation.

WARM-UP Begin the session with Body Sculpture Charades. Ask for three volunteers from the class. One will be the sculptor, and the other two will be the clay. Tell the students that the sculptor will sculpt a word out of the human clay, and they will need to guess the word. Try using the following words: *friendship, fighting, curiosity, play, forgiveness.* (Make sure that *forgiveness* is the last word you use.) Whisper a word to the sculptor and ask him/her to mold the clay in ways that will depict the word. When each body sculpture is complete, have the rest of the class guess the word depicted. Repeat this exercise several times with different words and different groups.

ACTIVITY Prior to the session, print on a piece of poster board the entire answer to "What is the benefit of such eating and drinking?" from page 50 of the *A Contemporary Translation of Luther's Small Catechism.* Then cut the answer into a number of separate poster board strips—so that each participant will have one strip. Write the question on a chalkboard; then randomly post strips of poster board around the room.

Have each person take one of the strips. Ask them to hold their strips in front of them and then arrange themselves in the correct order so that the catechism's answer appears. (They can use their catechisms, if need be.)

Now have them look at the words/phrases on their tagboard strips. Ask, "What words or phrases are most important for understanding the gifts we receive in Holy Communion?" Challenge the group to choose three words/phrases, and write them on the chalkboard below the question. *(One of these words needs to be* forgiveness.*)*

Duplicate Reproducible Page 8 and cut the copies apart. Now ask two pairs of students to perform the two role plays described there. Then lead a discussion of the questions on the "Observer's Sheet" portion of that sheet. Then ask the students to read aloud once again the second section of "The Sacrament of Holy Communion" on page 50 of *A Contemporary Translation of Luther's Small Catechism.* Ask class members to tell, in light of the two role plays, why it is true that where there is forgiveness of sins, there is also life and salvation.

RESPONSE Ask each class member to write a short letter to someone with whom he or she is angry or from who he or she is estranged. The letters should reflect what has been learned about forgiveness in today's session. Challenge group members to consider using the letter as a vehicle of forgiveness (to give or seek forgiveness from the other person). Tell them that they don't have to mail or deliver their letters, although they may wish to do so.

---

1. From *Free to Be: A Handbook to Luther's Small Catechism* (rev. ed.) by James A. Nestingen and Gerhard O. Forde, copyright © 1993 Augsburg Fortress.

Sacraments: Baptism and Holy Communion
"For You" Faith

FOCUS   The faith that the sacrament creates opens our hearts to receive the sacrament's gifts.

BACKGROUND   The anxiety some believers have had about going to Holy Communion has all too often prevented them from tasting the sacrament's goodness. "When is someone ready to receive such a great gift?" we might ask. If we respond to that question solely on the basis of our attitudes or our actions, we will never be ready. The Small Catechism, however, directs us away from ourselves and toward God. God's liberating promise—"for you"—creates in us the faith we need to receive the sacrament rightly.

WARM-UP   Ask the young people to find partners. One person covers or closes his or her eyes; the other person serves as guide on the tour the group will take together. It is each guide's responsibility to see that his or her partner remains with the group and is safe at all times.

Lead the entire group on a walk throughout the church building, returning to your class area. (Avoid barriers, like steps.) Invite the group members to remove their blindfolds and sit in a circle. Discuss two questions: What was the hardest task for the "guides"? What helped the guided ones to trust their guides?

ACTIVITY   Before the session, write one of the following statements of each note card; divide the cards and make sure one-third of the students will receive each comment:

1. I've done something so horrible that I don't know if even God will forgive me.

2. I never feel any different after I go to the Lord's Supper.

3. I just go to the Lord's Supper because my parents expect me to go.

Ask the group to turn to page 50 in *A Con-temporary Translation of Luther's Small Cate-chism* and read the third and fourth sections of "The Sacrament of Holy Communion." Then hand each participant a note card. Ask them to imagine that one of their friends has made this particular comment to them. Based on what they know about Holy Communion (especially in these last two sections on Holy Communion in the catechism), how might they respond to their friend?

When people have had time to think about this individually, ask them to find all the other people with the same comment on their card. Give the three groups time to discuss their responses and select one response they think is best. Then let each group share their comment and response with the entire class.

RESPONSE   Divide into two teams for a Point/Counterpoint discussion. Inform them that you will be reading a series of opinions about Holy Communion. After each statement is read, one team will huddle together and come up with reasons to *agree* with the statement; the other team will huddle and come up with reasons to *disagree*. Each team will choose a spokesperson to speak for the team in the discussion. Use the following opinion statements:

1. Because Holy Communion is so important to Christians, it should be reserved for special occasions only, and not celebrated every Sunday.

2. If someone has a weak faith, he or she should probably not come to Holy Communion.

3. The age at which persons can first come to Communion should be lowered in our congregation.

4. You get *out* of Holy Communion what you put *into* it.

Office of the Keys

FOCUS Jesus gave to the whole church (and that includes us) one of the keys to life: the gift of being able to forgive another.

BACKGROUND A congregation calls a pastor to teach; do pastoral ministry; lead worship; and officiate at baptisms, funerals, and weddings so all of these things will be done in an orderly fashion. Yet, Jesus gave everyone who is baptized the gift of being able to declare the forgiveness of sins to one another. This gift is referred to as the "Office of the Keys."

Martin Luther did not write the "Office of the Keys." However, it is included in many earlier editions of the Small Catechism, and it addresses a key element of Lutheran faith and life: God's forgiveness of sins and our ability to forgive one another.

The Office of the Keys

What is the "Office of the Keys"?

It is that authority which Christ gave to his church to forgive the sins of those who repent and to declare to those who do not repent that their sins are not forgiven.

What are the words of Christ?

Our Lord Jesus Christ said to his disciples: "Receive the Holy Spirit. If you forgive the sins of any, they are forgiven them; if you retain the sins of any, they are retained."—John 20:22b-23

"Truly I tell you, whatever you bind on earth will be bound in heaven, and whatever you loose on earth will be loosed in heaven."—Matthew 18:18

From *The Small Catechism by Martin Luther in Contemporary English* (1979 ed.), copyright © 1960, 1968 Augsburg Publishing House, Board of Publication of the Lutheran Church in America, Concordia Publishing House.

◆ Reproducible Page 11 may be used with this session on the Office of the Keys.

WARM-UP Gather and distribute at least one key for each person and ask the group to examine them closely. Have them use their imaginations. What might each key open? Read the first part of the "Office of the Keys" to the group. Have volunteers read aloud John 20:22b-23 and Matthew 18:18.

ACTIVITY Each person may use the key handed to them in the previous activity. Give each one a piece of paper and a pencil, and ask him or her to trace the outline of the key near the top of the paper. Invite everyone to think of important keys they may receive in their lifetime. Have them describe each of those keys in a simple phrase or sentence.

Now ask them think to think of figurative keys they hope to have. For example, Jesus said he was giving his followers "the keys to the kingdom of heaven." This refers to the key of forgiveness. With this key, new relationships can be opened between persons.

RESPONSE Read John 20:22-23. Then ask: Is this gift given to each of us? *(Yes.)* How can this gift of the ability to forgive another person be called a *key* to life? *(With the ability to restore broken relationships, our life and the live of others can be filled with harmony and happiness.)*

Distribute copies of *Lutheran Book of Worship.* Invite the students to open them to page 193. Point out the title "Corporate Confession and Forgiveness" at the top of the page. Ask them to turn to rubric 10 on the next page. Here it is suggested that the minister say the words of forgiveness while laying hands on a person's head.

Invite students to come to you with their worship books open to page 194. Kneel or sit and have each place a hand on your head or shoulder. Confess to them, by saying, "I am not as faithful in prayer as I should be; I have failed to be all God wants me to be" or some other confession. Then ask the students to read in unison the declaration of forgiveness in rubric 10 while they keep their hands on your head or shoulder. *("In obedience to the command of our Lord Jesus Christ, I forgive you all your sins.")*

See corresponding activity in the *Youth Journal*, page 51.

Welcome to Martin's World

Putting yourself in someone else's shoes helps you understand why that person thought, felt, and acted like he or she did. So, together, you are going to re-create the world in which Martin Luther lived. This experience can be as simple or complicated as you want to make it.

You can have fun together within your meeting space and limit your activities to a small portion of class time; or, you can invite the rest of your congregation to join you in staging a real "Reformation" event that wraps itself around your entire church property!

You can get by with a few resource books and your healthy imaginations; or, you can build a medieval village, fill it with the sounds, sights, and smells that Luther knew, and see what Martin's shoes feel like on your feet!

DIRECTIONS: *As you plan your experience, find ways to help participants answer these questions.*

1. When and where did Martin Luther live?

2. What kind of clothes did people wear?

3. What kind of homes did people have?

4. What kind of food did people eat?

5. What health problems were the most bothersome?

6. How did the government affect people's lives?

7. What role did the church play in people's lives?

8. How did adults and children spend their daily lives?

9. What role did violence play in the community life?

10. Who were the most powerful people in the community?

11. What roles were assigned to men and to women?

12. What was an indulgence?

13. What happened at the Diet of Worms?

Teaching the Truth

Martin Luther's spark of protest soon grew into a roaring inferno. In 1521, Luther was called to the German city of Worms and asked to denounce his teaching. Luther refused and narrowly escaped with his life. He was declared an enemy of the Roman Catholic Church and a price was put on his head. However, Luther's arguments about Christ's all-sufficient victory on the cross and the inability of men and women to save themselves made sense to a large number of people. Furthermore, the people were tired of the way bishops and other clergy seemed to be enriching themselves while their poor parishioners remained uncertain about their final destiny. Consequently, Luther was protected and the movement gained steam. Centered in Wittenberg, Luther and his followers preached, wrote, and taught about Christ's love for the ungodly. By the 1530s, wide areas of northern Europe were won over to the Lutheran faith.

A final attempt to heal the breach between Luther's followers and Rome occurred at the German city of Augsburg in 1530. However, by this time the two sides were too far apart. One result of this meeting was the Augsburg Confession, a summary of the Lutheran understanding of the Bible that remains authoritative for Lutherans today. Luther himself lived out his later years preaching and teaching the gospel and urging the reform of the church in accordance with God's Word. He was married in 1525 to Katherine von Bora, a former nun. They had six children together. He died in 1546 and is generally recognized to be one of the most influential people in history.

The Basics of Faith

Martin Luther wrote many books, but the Small Catechism was one of his favorites. The church bearing his name has echoed this sentiment and made the Small Catechism a staple of confirmation instruction for more than 400 years. Luther wrote this teaching tool in the late 1520s. When he visited some churches in the area of Wittenberg with other leaders of the Reformation, he saw that the common people were in desperate need of a basic guide to the Christian faith. So, he wrote the simple, yet elegant, Small Catechism.

Luther put the Ten Commandments first, followed by the Apostles' Creed, the Lord's Prayer, and the Sacraments of Baptism and Holy Communion. This order reflected Luther's belief that through the Law, the Commandments, we learn to dismiss any possibility of saving ourselves. Once that is established, then we are ready to receive the mercy of Christ as contained in the Creed and the Lord's Prayer. The sacraments reinforce this by talking about how Christ comes in the midst of our daily lives and nurtures our faith.

Down through the ages the gentle rhythms of the Small Catechism have nurtured countless Christians in the fundamentals of the faith. Those who make it their own have a companion to treasure until they are reunited with Christ.

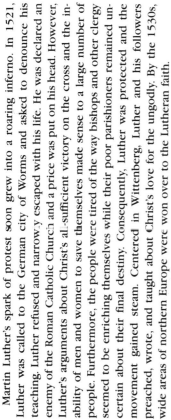

A Need for Reform

In 1500, the continent of Europe was dramatically different from the one we know today. Frightful diseases were common; during the 14th century, the plague wiped out almost half of Europe's population. If a person was fortunate enough to survive childbirth, she could expect to live only to the age of 40. Only a small percentage of people could read.

The Roman Catholic Church was the only church of significance. This powerful church was headed by the pope; yet, many cracks and strains were beginning to exist beneath its polished surface. Its basic problem was related to a controversy about salvation.

Late medieval theology taught that it was up to the individual to initiate a saving relationship with God. As a result, men and women were left wondering whether they had "done enough" to satisfy God. For those with sensitive consciences—and their number was not small—this led to a piety that sought to "do something" (like fasting or taking a pilgrimage) to become right with God.

God's Forgiveness

Martin Luther was born in Germany in 1483. After completing his early studies, Luther began preparing to be a lawyer, largely at the urging of his father. A near-death experience in a thunderstorm in 1505 led Luther to enter a monastery. While there, Luther began his lifelong study of Scripture. He earned his doctor's degree in theology in 1512. As a monk, Luther's chief concern was to save himself.

The church of the day taught that a person must at least initiate a relationship with God before God would bestow the grace necessary to save. This teaching tormented the conscientious Luther. Luther felt he had never done enough to merit God's love and favor, no matter how much he fasted, read the Bible, or confessed his sins. Driven to the edge of despair, Luther discovered in the Bible that God's love exists prior to any of our good works. Jesus Christ died to forgive our sins and that act alone is sufficient to warrant our inclusion in God's kingdom. In particular, he found Paul's teaching that we are justified by faith and not by works of the law to be tremendously freeing.

Armed with this new understanding of Christ and God's Word, Luther challenged the view of the established church in Rome. In 1517, he nailed his 95 theses to the door of the church in Wittenberg, the university town where he was teaching. He declared that the Roman church's selling of indulgences (slips of paper that forgave sins) was contrary to Scripture. Many people, especially in Germany, agreed with Luther. A significant movement to renew the church was born. We know that movement as the Reformation.

Directions: This background information can be used in conjunction with the activities in the "Catechism Basics" unit or with those who need to work independently. It duplicates some of the information on pages 4-7 in this leader guide. More information is available in the introductory pages of *A Contemporary Translation of Luther's Small Catechism: Study Edition.*

Reproducible Page 2 ◆ Small Catechism

Do you move like an amoeba?

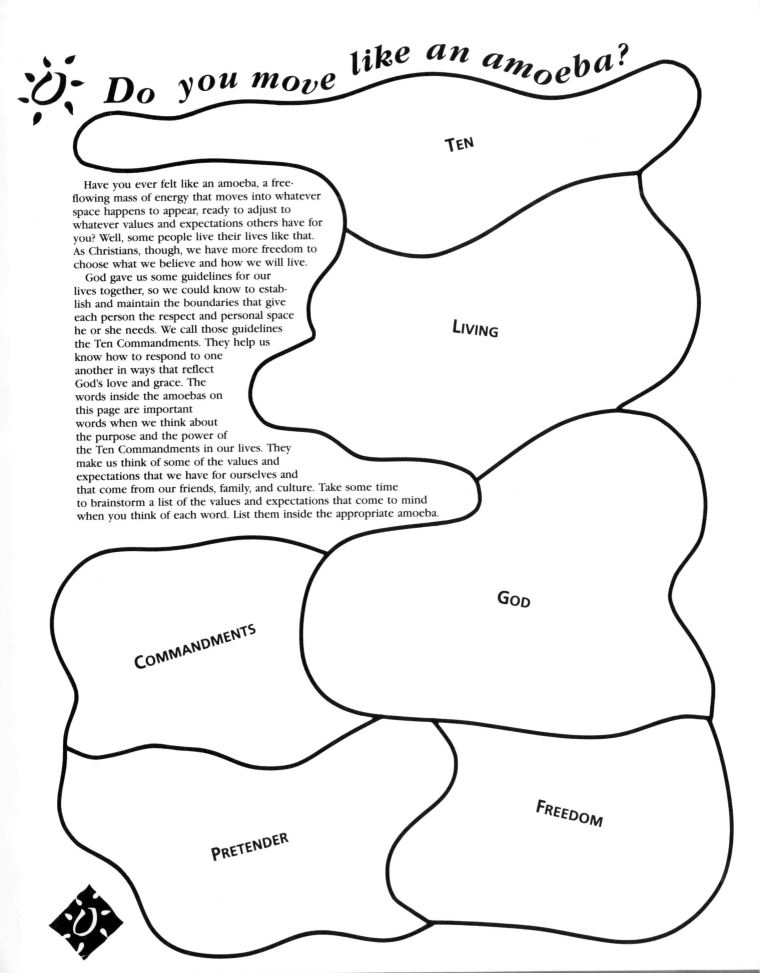

TEN

Have you ever felt like an amoeba, a free-flowing mass of energy that moves into whatever space happens to appear, ready to adjust to whatever values and expectations others have for you? Well, some people live their lives like that. As Christians, though, we have more freedom to choose what we believe and how we will live.

God gave us some guidelines for our lives together, so we could know to establish and maintain the boundaries that give each person the respect and personal space he or she needs. We call those guidelines the Ten Commandments. They help us know how to respond to one another in ways that reflect God's love and grace. The words inside the amoebas on this page are important words when we think about the purpose and the power of the Ten Commandments in our lives. They make us think of some of the values and expectations that we have for ourselves and that come from our friends, family, and culture. Take some time to brainstorm a list of the values and expectations that come to mind when you think of each word. List them inside the appropriate amoeba.

LIVING

GOD

COMMANDMENTS

FREEDOM

PRETENDER

Time Bucks

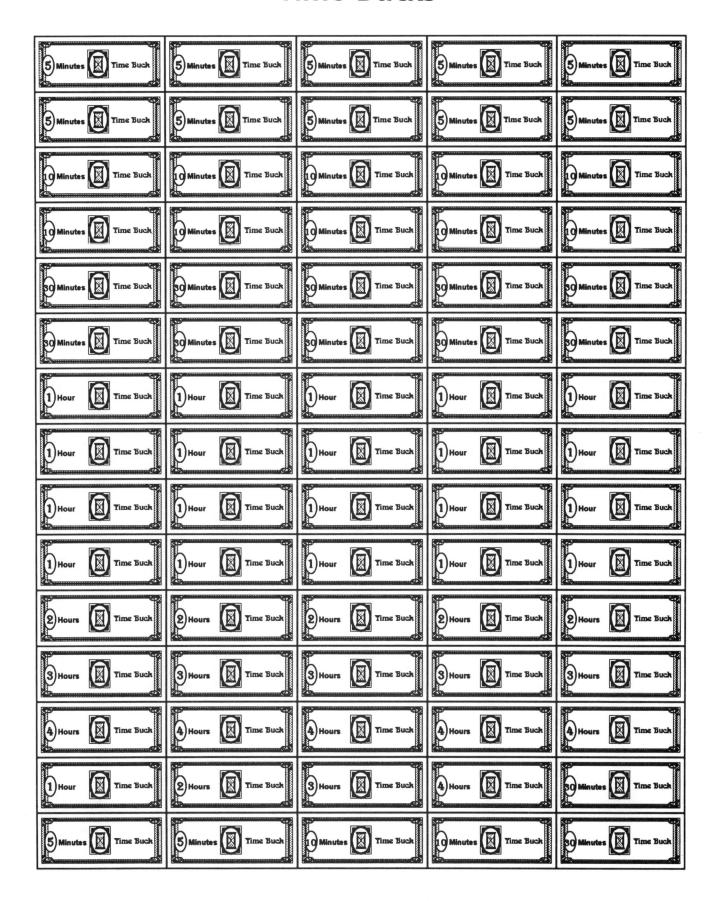

Ephesians 4:25—5:2

So then, putting away falsehood, let all of us speak the truth to our neighbors, for we are members of one another. Be angry but do not sin; do not let the sun go down on your anger, and do not make room for the devil. Thieves must give up stealing; rather let them labor and work honestly with their own hands, so as to have something to share with the needy. Let no evil talk come out of your mouths, but only what is useful for building up, as there is need, so that your words may give grace to those who hear. And do not grieve the Holy Spirit of God, with which you were marked with a seal for the day of redemption. Put away from you all bitterness and wrath and anger and wrangling and slander, together with all malice, and be kind to one another, tenderhearted, forgiving one another, as God in Christ has forgiven you.

Therefore, be imitators of God as beloved children, and live in love, as Christ loved us and gave himself for us, a fragrant offering and sacrifice to God.

Ephesians 4:25—5:2

So then, putting away _ _ _ _ _ _ _ _, let all of us speak the truth to our neighbors, for we are members of one another. Be angry but do not sin; do not let the sun go down on your anger, and do not make room for the devil. Thieves must give up stealing; rather let them labor and work honestly with their own hands, so as to have something to share with the needy. Let no _ _ _ _ _ _ _ _ come out of your mouths, but only what is useful for building up, as there is need, so that your words may give grace to those who hear. And do not _ _ _ _ _ _ the Holy Spirit of God, with which you were marked with a seal for the day of redemption. Put away from you all bitterness and wrath and anger and wrangling and slander, together with all malice, and be kind to one another, tenderhearted, forgiving one another, as God in Christ has forgiven you.

Therefore, be _ _ _ _ _ _ _ _ _ _ _ _ _ _ as beloved children, and live in love, as Christ loved us and gave himself for us, a fragrant offering and sacrifice to God.

Find the Key Word

What one word comes to your mind when you think about the meaning of the Ninth Commandment? See if you can discover it by looking up these Bible verses and answering the following questions.

The answers are all numbers, and those numbers have been coded. Each numerical answer stands for a letter of the alphabet, such as: 1 = A. Find all the answers and then crack the code!

1		2		3		4		5		6		7	

1. How many people were killed when the tower fell? (Luke 13:4)

2. How many loaves did Jesus bless and break? (Mark 6:41)

3. How many towns are mentioned? (Joshua 19:38)

4. How old was King Azariah when he began to reign? (2 Kings 15:1-2)

5. How many bridesmaids were wise? (Matthew 25:2)

6. How many times did Jesus say Peter would deny him? (Matthew 26:34)

7. How many cubits long is the flying scroll? (Zechariah 5:2)

TO THE LEADER: Cover the following code when reproducing this page.

A	B	C	D	E	F	G	H	I	J	K	L	M	N	O	P	Q	R	S	T	U	V	W	X	Y	Z
1	2	3	4	5	6	7	8	9	10	11	12	13	14	15	16	17	18	19	20	21	22	23	24	25	26

The Story of Zacchaeus
Luke 19:1-10

BACKGROUND

In Jesus' day, **tax collectors** were Jewish persons who collected taxes for the Roman government. The Romans ruled the Jewish people during that time in history, and the Jewish people resented this foreign rule. Tax collectors were hated by the Jewish people for two reasons:

♦ They were viewed as traitors by their own people because they served the Romans.
♦ They frequently demanded too much money, keeping the extra portion for themselves and becoming rich in the process.

STORY

1. Read Luke 19:1-10 silently and then discuss the following question with the people in your small group: **Who plays the role of Zacchaeus in your community? What person or group of persons gets treated the way that Zacchaeus was treated?**

2. Create in your small group a modern version of the Zacchaeus story using the person or group your group selected as the contemporary counterpart for Zacchaeus as the main character(s). Have your story take place right in your own school building, involving people your own age. Decide how to make a short drama out of your story. *(For example, one of you will be the Zacchaeus figure, one of you will be the Christ figure, and others will be the crowd.)* After all groups have had time to prepare, your leader will ask each small group to perform its drama for the class.

REPENTANCE

We often think of repentance as feeling sorry about our sins and asking for forgiveness. Guilt is what motivates us to repent. In the Bible, however, repentance means much more than feeling guilty or sorry about what we have done. It involves *changing our minds* about something and looking at things in a whole new way. Instead of feeling guilty or bad about ourselves, repentance can be our joyful response to God's love and goodness. Persons who repent are so overcome by God's mercy that they willingly clear away whatever has been standing between them and God. Repentance opens them up to be ready to continue to receive God's promises. Discuss the following questions in your small groups:

1. In Luke 19:1-10 does Zacchaeus seem to repent because Jesus made him feel awful about himself, or does he repent because Jesus made him feel loved and accepted?

2. Can you think of a time when you or someone you know well repented (or changed their mind) the way Zacchaeus did? Please share this story with the people in your group.

Role Plays

DIRECTIONS: *Cut the role-play instructions apart and give them to the four class members who will be performing the role plays. Each person should see only his/her own role play instructions. The rest of the class members should each receive an "OBSERVER'S SHEET."*

ROLE PLAY 1: Toni & Sue

TONI: You did something terrible to your best friend, Sue. She was counting on you to go with her to last Friday night's game. You had even promised to meet at a certain time and walk to the game together. But something came up for you Friday evening, and you forgot your promise to Sue.

Sue's friendship really means a lot to you. In this role play, tell Sue (in as many different ways as you can) that you are truly sorry, and you will make sure that it won't happen again.

SUE: Your "friend" Toni has forgotten about a promise she made to you one too many times. She stood you up last Friday night, after you had specifically planned to go to the game together.

You are fed up with Toni. You've given her too many second chances already. You're tired of forgiving and forgetting. As far as you're concerned, your friendship is finished.

ROLE PLAY 2: Juan & Greg

JUAN: You and your classmate Greg have enjoyed doing lots of things together over the years. The one thing you can't figure out about Greg is why he doesn't go out for basketball. You've asked him to join you on the team a number of times, but he always brushes you off.

You're starting to wonder if he's some sort of wimp who doesn't want to work hard enough to make the team. In this role play, you really push Greg to join the team and prove himself. You get involved in a big argument and wind up walking away from each other.

GREG: Juan is someone you've considered to be a friend for a long time. But lately he's been bugging you about going out for the basketball team—even though you can't stand basketball. Juan is even starting to imply that you aren't tough enough to be on a sports team.

In this role play, you tell Juan that you want nothing to do with basketball. If he can't drop the subject, you no longer want to have anything to do with him. The two of you wind up in an argument—and, in anger, you walk away from each other.

OBSERVER'S SHEET

As you observe the two role plays, think about and be ready to discuss the following questions.

1. How do you think each character might have felt?

2. What obstacles stand between the characters?

3. What kind of future do Sue and Toni or Juan and Greg have with one another?

4. What does each relationship need for it to survive?

Prayer

We learn about prayer from talking to others, from the Bible, from reading and listening to prayers written by others, and from praying. After you have studied each petition of the Lord's Prayer, complete the corresponding prayer in this folder and make it your own.

"The Jesus Prayer" is hundreds of years old. Christians across the ages have prayed it slowly, repeating it several times, stopping after each word or phrase to think what they mean. You may wish to pray this prayer each time you use this folder. You may wish to pray it silently, slowly, meditating on each word or phrase.

Lord, Jesus Christ, Son of God, have mercy, on me.

FIRST PETITION
Heavenly Father, I want to tell you how I feel about you today. Father I . . .

Dear God, when I hear others use your name in bad ways help me . . .

SECOND PETITION
Strong God, while your powerful rule has already begun upon earth I'd like you to help me be a part of that rule by . . .

Kind God, when I see people who need help, use me to bring them . .

THIRD PETITION
O God, there are times when I feel evil forces are operating against those things you want to happen among your people. Use your power in those times to . . .

Loving God, when bad things happen to good people remind me that . . .

FOURTH PETITION
Creator God, I am especially thankful this day for . . . Kind God, I really want to have a thankful heart at all times because . . .

FIFTH PETITION
Forgiving God, let my awareness of your forgiveness of my sins motivate me to forgive _____ by . . .

Dear God, I want to remember the following people in prayer: _____ and ask that you would bless them with the knowledge you are ready to forgive them . . .

SIXTH PETITION
O God, there are so many traps in my life into which I could easily fall. Open my eyes to see those traps and . . .

Lord Jesus, it was easy to eagerly sing "Jesus loves me this I know" when I was young. Now I wonder if I will be loyal to you when the going gets tough. Help me . . .

SEVENTH PETITION
Lord, my shepherd, when I get scared because of wicked and evil things in our world, help me remember . . .

Jesus, when you were dying on the cross, you prayed words from one of the psalms, words every Jewish mother taught her children to pray: "Father, into your hands I commend my spirit" (Luke 23:46). Help me to pray this prayer when . . .

NOTE TO THE LEADER: *Ask your church secretary for some extra bulletin covers that relate to prayer. Reproduce this sheet on the inside of those covers so the students can keep this folder as a special memento of their study of the Lord's Prayer.*

Adventure and Challenges Game

When we pray the Third Petition of the Lord's Prayer, we are reminded that God hears our prayers when we are struggling with the daily challenges of being a faithful follower of Jesus. It reminds us that we need to trust God to be with us in all of our experiences and give us the wisdom, strength, and courage to endure.

As you play this game, remember that God provides for our needs—no matter what kind of adventures we face. We may have to take a second look at the resources we have within us or within the community of faith to which we belong, but we will find what we need to meet the challenges of our daily lives.

1. Assign each of these POWER characteristics to one person in the group. If there are fewer than 10 persons in the group, assign more than one characteristic to some of them. If there are more than 10 persons in the group, have the others decide which person has the power to handle the particular adventure or challenge as it occurs in the story. When each characteristic is needed, the appropriate person should step forward. Try to use everyone's power at least once during the game.

- ◆ Person with gymnastic ability
- ◆ Person with ability to size up the situation
- ◆ Person with compassion and soothing spirit
- ◆ Person with general medical knowledge
- ◆ Person who is bold and also polite
- ◆ Person carrying heavy rope and metal anchor
- ◆ Person with survival training
- ◆ Person with good sense of direction
- ◆ Person with experience cutting branches
- ◆ Person with clever mind

2. Begin the game by reading this script aloud:

We are living in Europe during the Middle Ages. We are a troop of adventurers who are looking for a specific castle. We know what general area the castle is in, but we do not know its exact location. The terrain is rough, and the footing is unsure. *Who will lead the way?*

One member of the troop turns an ankle on a tree root and is in great pain. That person can't continue walking. *How can the person continue on the journey?*

A storm suddenly hits. *Where can the group take shelter?*

Huddled under a bridge for protection, some strange creatures begin hurling stones upon the group. Two more persons are injured and are treated. *How will the rest of the group be calmed down so we can continue on the journey to the castle?*

Emerging from a heavily forested terrain, the group comes upon a grassy plain surrounded by rock covered steep hills on three sides. There is no path to follow. Night comes and the howls of wild animals fill the air. We discover our provisions have been left behind. *What will we eat? Where shall the group spend the night?*

A horde of bats fly out of a nearby cave some members of the troop try to enter. A person becomes frightened, runs, falls and hurts his shoulder. The night is cold. *How can a fire be started in such a desolate place?*

In the morning, the group presses forward to the top of the hills ahead. *Who helps those who are afraid of climbing?*

The other side of the hills are densely forested, and the vegetation makes it impossible to move with any speed. *How can we find a path in the vegetation?*

The castle is spotted. But a wide, deep moat filled with water and alligators surrounds the castle, and the drawbridge is up. *How can the castle be entered?*

Inside the castle, someone in the group discovers a host has prepared a banquet for them. To enter the banquet, troop members must have a special wedding garment. Obviously, no one in the group is carrying such a garment. *Who will solve this problem?*

The banquet is ready. All of us enter. Some of us have been injured, and we have all faced threatening danger and evil. Yet, we have arrived at our destination and are ready to celebrate a wedding feast with the most gracious host in the kingdom. *Who will give thanks?*

Where do you stand?

DIRECTIONS: *Mark a clear path between two facing walls and run a rope along it. Label one wall with a sign that says I AGREE; label the other wall with a sign that says I DISAGREE.*

Are you a forgiving person? Jesus gave to the whole church (and that includes us) one of the keys to life: the gift of being able to forgive one another. Let's find out how forgiving we are.

Begin by standing in the middle of the room, away from the path. As each statement is read aloud, move to a place on the path that reflects your experience with it. After you have had a chance to notice where you have chosen to stand and its relationship to the positions taken by your classmates, move back to the center of the room.

1. Forgiving someone else makes me feel better physically.

2. Some people do things that are too terrible to be forgiven.

3. I'm more likely to be forgiving when I'm around others who are forgiving.

4. It is more difficult for me to accept forgiveness than it is for me to forgive.

5. I can forgive, but I can never forget.

6. Being forgiving affects a person's mental and physical health.

7. Being unforgiving affects a person's mental and physical health.

8. I am more likely to get angry with people when they change the rules, instead of asking them why the rules were changed.

9. Sin is a part of human nature.

10. Every action a person takes is either right or wrong; circumstances do not make a difference.

11. It is a greater sin to break the rules of society than to ignore the needs of others.

12. My role as a Christian is to reflect God's forgiving love to others.

Reproducible Page 11 ◆ Small Catechism

To be used with "Office of the Keys," page 37. Creative Confirmation, copyright © 1994 Augsburg Fortress.
Permission is granted to reproduce this page provided that copies are for local use only and that each copy carries this copyright notice.